CABINET OFFIC
OFFICE of the MINIS⌐
for the CIVIL SERVIᴄᴇ

Understanding Stress:

Part Three

Trainer's Guide

London
Her Majesty's Stationery Office

ISBN 0 11 430021 6

Contents

Introduction

This book has been prepared for the Training Division of the Cabinet Office (OMCS) as part of the *Understanding Stress series.*

The series consists of four books:

- *Understanding Stress – Part One*
- *Understanding Stress – Part Two: Line Manager's Guide*
- *Understanding Stress – Part Three: Trainer's Guide*
- *Understanding Stress – Part Four: Welfare Officer's Guide*

The series has been produced as a resource and working tool to assist all those who have an interest in stress, either from their own point of view or from the point of view of someone who works with or manages other people.

Background

Stress as a likely cause of illness, problems and personal misery is giving rise to growing public as well as medical and scientific concern.

It is fair to say that at this point the complete scientific and clinical link between stress and illness has not been proved to the satisfaction of all parties. Despite this there is a growing realization that stress is an increasing problem.

The Economist noted that Britain is losing two per cent of its GNP per annum as a result of losses caused by stress-related diseases. This is a staggering figure which does not include less measurable costs such as human misery, lower efficiency and productivity.

In 1978 it was reported that Britain had one of the worst death rates from heart disease and strokes in the world – they account for 80,000 premature deaths per year.

About this book

This book is written for the non-specialist Trainer. It does not provide help in tackling deep-rooted problems like chronic anxiety or low self-esteem. Psychotherapy is highly skilled and is not the province of the non-specialist. Further skilled help will be needed for serious cases.

The material in this book is designed to:

- define stress briefly
- examine the role the Trainer can play in informing people about stress and helping them to control and manage it
- provide examples of programmes and resource materials which can be used to design and run training and information events
- provide information about relevant initiatives and studies in the area of stress
- give details of:
  - relevant training materials
  - useful organizations and individuals
  - further reading and information sources

Using this book

This book can be used on its own but will be more valuable if used alongside the book *Understanding Stress – Part One* which provides detailed information about stress and can be used as:

- self-instruction material
- a source of questionnaires and checklists which can be used to identify personal or work-based stressors
- a source of references for directed further reading

What's in it for the Trainer

The material in this book is arranged in four sections.

Section 1. The Trainer and stress management training

This section sets the scene and examines the Trainer's role in stress management and prevention.

Section 2. Sample training programmes

A selection of programmes for events relating to stress are included. These examples originate from a variety of Civil Service departments and outside organizations. You can use these examples either as models for events you need to run or as a source of ideas on the design and control of training events.

Section 3. Resource training material

This section contains a number of sample handouts and examples of overhead projector slides which have been developed by various departments and organizations.

The material is presented under four headings and will augment the information available in the book *Understanding Stress – Part One*

- What is stress?
- Symptoms of stress
- Causes of stress
- Managing stress

Section 4. Further sources of help

This section provides details of other help and advice available to Trainers and:

- lists useful organizations/individuals
- gives details of training materials and aids available

Section 5. Bibliography and research studies

Acknowledgements

This and the other three books in the series *Understanding Stress* were developed for the Training Division of the Cabinet Office (OMCS) by Diane Bailey and Clare Sproston of Diane Bailey Associates, 4 Rochbury Close, Bamford, Rochdale OL11 5JF.

The authors would like to thank the following who helped them in preparing the series *Understanding Stress* by providing information and advice and giving permission to include material:

Trainers, Welfare Officers and others in Civil Service departments

Chief Superintendent Allison, New Scotland Yard
Angela Stern Associates
Meg Bond and James Kilty, University of Surrey
City Relaxation Counselling
Eleanor MacDonald Courses Ltd
Industrial Society (Pepperell Unit)
Jean Jackson
Murray Giles Associates
Dr Nimenko, Devonshire Clinic
Alistair Ostell, Occupational Psychology Management Centre, Bradford University
Rank-Xerox
Rochdale Health Authority
Dr Adrian Semmence, Civil Service Occupational Health Service
Stress Foundation

Special thanks to those departments who helped by sharing the development costs of the series:

Ministry of Agriculture, Fisheries and Food
Cabinet Office (OMCS) – Training Division and Personnel Management Division 2
Civil Service College
Department of Education and Science
Department of Employment
Department of Employment (Unemployment Benefit Service)
Office of Fair Trading
Foreign and Commonwealth Office
Department of Health and Social Security
Department of National Savings
HM Land Registry
Inland Revenue
Lord Chancellor's Department
National Environment Research Council
Office of Population Censuses and Surveys
Science and Engineering Research Council
Welsh Office

Section 1
The Trainer and stress management training

Contents

What is stress?

Throughout this book and others in the series *Understanding Stress* the word 'stress' is used in the sense of the 'distress' which people experience from too many or too few pressures and strains. Distress is something which occurs to all of us, as does happiness. It is only when there is too much distress, physical or mental, that problems start.

The extent of the problem

Stress has recently become a very fashionable term and there is an increasing level of interest in it. Information available today suggests that something like 40 million work days are lost a year in the United Kingdom from illnesses which are in some way related to stress. For obvious reasons precise costing of the effects of this loss is difficult although a figure of £3,000 million has been suggested.

There is a high degree of similarity in the rates of stress identified by both commercial and community studies. A study carried out in the Home Office in the early 1980s* showed that the prevalent rate of 'inner psychiatric morbidity', one aspect of stress, among Executive Officers was more than 30 per cent. A year later, when the same sample was assessed, only 50 per cent of those involved had recovered. While it is hard to generalize from one study it is reasonable to suppose that similar results could be found elsewhere.

It makes sense to consider how to help people understand and cope with stress for their own sake, for the sake of the department or organization and for your own sake as a Line Manager working with people to achieve results and carry out tasks.

---

*JENKINS, R. 'Inner psychiatric morbidity in employed young men and women and its contribution to sickness absence'. *British Journal of Industrial Medicine.* Vol. 42, No. 3. 1985.

Stress at work

There is an intention in the Health and Safety at Work Act 1974 to include safeguards to mental as well as physical aspects of health. Despite this, in Britain to date most attention has been devoted to physical health and safety. In Scandinavia and America more attention has been paid to psychological stress, both generally and at work. In fact a number of US companies have had claims made against them for damage to mental health.

Admittedly it may be difficult to relate non-physical illnesses directly to specific work factors. But does this really matter? It makes sense to deal with stress at work as much because of cost considerations as because of the wider issues of caring for people and their comfort.

Role of the Trainer

As an organization becomes involved in dealing with stress it is logical that Trainers and the training department in general should contribute to identifying stress and, helping to manage and prevent it.

To be effective the contribution of Trainers needs to be part of a concerted effort rather then a series of disconnected initiatives. The ideal support system would be:

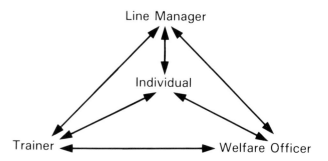

The model describes a situation where Trainers work with Line Managers, Welfare Officers and other Personnel Officers to provide a complete, integrated system designed to identify, manage and prevent stress. Good 'non-stress' training can, in itself, reduce stress in that the provision of appropriate skills and adequate knowledge equips people for their work and reduces one set of pressures.

Training and stress

Because the causes and effects of stress for each individual are many and different it is sensible for you as a Trainer to consider stress problems from three different angles:

- the individual
- their occupation
- the organization

The three-level approach is necessary if you want to look at individual problems in an appropriate context and identify the most appropriate solutions. Also, if you want to develop and plan preventative strategies, you will need the wider perspective. Additionally, by attempting to tackle the problem at all three levels, you will find it easier and more logical to enlist the help of managers in varying parts of the organization and to make best use of the welfare and personnel function's experience and resources.

Providing stress management training

The type of stress training you need and can provide and the backdrop against which you provide it will depend on:

- the size, organization and philosophy of your department or organization
- its approach to and acceptance of stress as a legitimate area of training activity
- whether your own role as trainer is seen as reactive, interventionist or proactive
- your own level of knowledge and skill
- how *you* view your role
- whether you are dealing with problems of the individual or the organization
- how closely you can liaise with line management and personnel
- how well specific training needs have been identified
- the resources available to you

Training needs

Training needs in the area of stress which you may need to resource could include:

- straight information sessions about the definition and causes of stress for management, or other groups of staff
- specific courses or workshops designed to:
  - identify causes of stress
  - examine organizational stresses
  - develop coping and stress management skills
- specific events to help managers examine how occupational and work stresses can be reduced/modified
- input sessions on stress on general supervisory or management courses
- identifying further sources of help and information

Only you can know exactly what present circumstances demand of you or what you would like to do.

Your personal involvement

It would be useful at this point for you to spend a little time in thinking about some of the factors already mentioned so that you can get a clearer picture of your possible involvement in stress training. Answer the questions below.

What is my department or organization's view of stress as a legitimate area of training activity?

_____

_____

_____

Are there any 'attitudes' which need to be changed or circumvented?

_____

_____

_____

If so, how can I achieve what is necessary?

_____

_____

_____

Am I expected to be purely reactive or is some/any degree of intervention or proaction expected/required of me?

_____

_____

_____

What do I have to deal with – the problems of the individual, or the organization, or both?

_____

_____

_____

How good is my co-operation with line management?

_____

_____

_____

How good is my co-operation with the personnel/welfare department?

_____

_____

_____

What limitations do I see in my own skills?

_____

_____

_____

How can I correct these?

_____

_____

_____

Have specific stress training needs been identified?

_____

_____

_____

If not, can I identify any which need to be filled?

_____

_____

_____

Have I sufficient resources?

_____

_____

_____

If not, how can I get them?

_____

_____

_____

What outside/specialist help will I need?

_____

_____

Do I make the most of the help and support available from line management and the welfare/personnel service?

_____

_____

_____

Am I aware of other sources of help and information?

_____

_____

_____

Once you have considered and answered these questions you will have a closer understanding of what is expected and what is possible at present in your department or organization.

What is happening elsewhere

A small survey conducted as part of a wider research programme at the Stress Research and Control Centre* looked at how stress was dealt with in 35 large UK companies. All companies in the sample provided training for different levels of employee.

In the sample of firms surveyed almost half of them had run a short course or workshop on stress management within the previous two years. In some cases the events had been set up by the welfare department or medical section. In only a small proportion of cases was the workshop a discrete entity. In most cases the stress training was part of a wider training programme or one session in a training event.

Nearly three-quarters of events identified during the survey were aimed at middle and senior management. There is no evidence to indicate that managers are more at risk than any other group but there are several reasons why they might be seen as a good place to start.

- Managers are highly visible
- Management costs tend to be higher than those of other groups
- Managers can (and often do) delegate stress to other groups
- Without management commitment and acceptance no stress training initiative can be successful
- There may be hope of a cascade effect from managers who are more aware of the problems of stress
- It may be politically more acceptable to offer courses which are seen to be concerned with identifying and managing stress for others

---

*A survey of stress management and prevention facilities in a sample of UK organizations. Stress Research and Control Centre, Birkbeck College, London. 1983.

Organizing stress management training

If you have carried out the brief analysis on pages 6 to 8 you will now have some idea of the precise situation in which you have to work. Obviously the sixteen questions in that analysis cannot provide all the information you need, but answering them will give you a good start.

Your work in stress training will involve you in:
- defining the problem
- identifying action for others to take
- taking action yourself

Defining the problem

You will be involved in several types of definition:
- overviews and perspectives of stress for managers and general groups
- working with groups or individuals to help them identify causes of stress and symptoms to be watched for

If you are working with groups, the discussion may be abstract or very general rather than concerned with an individual's problems. In one-to-one or informal group situations you may have to manage very personal discussions. You will need to make sure that you can cope with the emotions expressed.

In either kind of discussion you need to be positive. Avoid letting a discussion degenerate into moaning, focus as far as possible on productive discussion and on trying to identify realistic, achievable objectives for change or coping.

Identifying and taking action

Desirable action to be taken will differ with each individual or group because the causes of stress will differ. In your groups you will be identifying two or more sorts of necessary action:
- that which can be taken by the individual or the group

- that which must be taken by someone else either inside the department, or even outside it

Your role will be two-fold; to help individuals and groups identify and plan to take action for themselves, and to act as go-between when desirable action is needed from elsewhere.

Skills needed

Working in the area of stress is a delicate operation. You will be dealing with people at a very real and sensitive level. Do not blunder in where a little knowledge could be dangerous.

Define carefully the limits of your activities and those areas which must be left for the specialist. Remember that as a trainer you are very much a facilitator and that your role could very usefully be to deal with the general while involving other people/bodies to deal with particular problems.

Group work and detailed one-to-one counselling are skilled tasks. This book is *not* designed to equip you with these skills. It is sensible before you begin to work with stress to take stock of your experience and skills and to arrange help if you think you need it.

Skills required for group work include:

- defining aims and objectives
- a high level of interpersonal skill and credibility
- planning and designing effective sessions
- controlling (but not directing) discussion
- dealing with awkward or troubled individuals
- helping people find solutions to their own problems

Skills needed for dealing with individuals will include:

- dealing with a range of emotional reactions including anger
- encouraging people
- identifying blocks and obstacles
- getting past these blocks and obstacles
- staying reasonably detached and objective
- problem solving

Getting help

If you want to improve your skills or get further help, Section 4 of this book gives details of useful organizations and training materials.

Potential problems

When getting ready to run training events concerned with stress there will be certain basic problems which could face you. These include:

- not being sufficiently informed on the subject of stress
- not having all the skills involved/required
- the climate in your department/organization which may make it difficult to accept/admit stress as a legitimate area of training activity
- the expections of trainees
- senior management may be sceptical
- individuals may fear to admit or discuss stress as it could be seen as a weakness
- contamination from a 'do-gooding' attitude
- previous failed attempts
- serious problem areas which should not be tackled by an amateur
- lack of support/understanding from line managers
- lack of clarity about organizational boundaries

Your problems

Before starting to design any training event, take time to define the problems which face you and to work out how best to overcome or get round them. Use the questions which follow to help you get your thoughts organized.

Do you know enough about the subject?

_____

If not, where can you find the information you need?

_____

_____

_____

Are you fully aware of and competent in the skills needed?

_____

_____

If not, where/when can you get the training you need?

_____

_____

Are there cynical/sceptical attitudes to overcome? If so specify them.

_____

_____

_____

What are the likely expectations of groups and individuals?

_____

_____

Can you overcome these on your own? Or do you need to bring in help?

_____

_____

_____

If you need help can you get it from within the department or organization? Or do you have to go outside?

_____

_____

If you need to go outside for help what is likely to be the best source?

_____

_____

_____

Your notes and other points to consider (note down anything which you wish to consider further).

_____

_____

_____

_____

_____

Designing a training event on stress

Once you have clarified the situation you can go on to design the specific training event. The checklist below will help you to get things organized.

Reason

1. Is the session/course to:
- inform?
- persuade?
- change attitude?
- develop skills?
- other? – specify

_____

2. What role are you being expected to play:
- reactive?
- interventionist?

_____

3. Have you initiated the training event?   yes/no

4. Has someone else requested it (eg managment)?   yes/no

5. Do the answers to questions 1 to 4 affect:
- the design of the training event?
- how you publicize it?
- where you hold it?
- who attends it?

- who runs it?
- any other factor?

_____

_____

6. What is your objective:
- to increase understanding?
- to change attitudes?
- to build skill?
- to provide practice in relaxation techniques?
- other? – specify.

_____

_____

7. What learning objective(s) should you set?

_____

_____

_____

8. Who is your target audience?

_____

_____

_____

9. What kind of problems, if any, could this present:
- organizational?
- political?

- timing?
- venue?
- balance of content?
- other? – specify.

_____

_____

10. What is the optimum number of participants?

_____

11. Content/subject matter. Are you dealing with:

- definition of stress?
- symptoms?
- causes?
- management and coping skills?
- a combination of any of these?

_____

_____

_____

12. Is there an existing programme?

- Do you have to design one?
- Do you have to have one designed?

_____

13. Do you know enough to cover the necessary content?   yes/no

14. If not – where can you find the expertise/ information?

_____

_____

15. How many tutors are needed?

_____

16. Are you going to run the event:

- on your own?
- with a colleague?
- with outside help?
- leave entirely to outsiders?

_____

_____

17. How long is the event to be?

_____

18. Over what period is it to be run?

_____

19. Are there likely to be any potential problems with:

- participants?
- publicity?
- finding the venue?
- finding the expertise?
- finding the material?
- finding the equipment?
- funding?
- other? – specify.

_____

_____

20. Are you sufficiently knowledgeable about the work environment of the trainees to relate the event specifically to the needs of the participants?   yes/no

21. Are you aware of stress factors in their environment?   yes/no

22. If no to questions 20 and 21 above – how do you get the relevant information?

_____

_____

_____

23. Are there any recent or forthcoming changes in the work environment of the participants?

_____

_____

_____

24. Do you need to liaise with Line Managers and/or Welfare Officers?   yes/no

25. Will the balance of:

- job roles
- sexes
- ethnic groups
- ages

lead to any special requirements or pre-course work?

_____

_____

_____

26. What is the best environment:
- in-house?
- external premises?
- head office?
- regional offices?

_____

27. How many rooms will be needed:
- one main room?
- one and syndicates?

_____

28. List any other factors you think relevant.

_____

_____

_____

Section 2.
Sample training programmes

Contents

Introduction

The purpose of this section is to provide examples of a number of training programmes that have been run successfully in Civil Service departments and outside organizations. The programmes which follow do not constitute an exhaustive list but rather are chosen to provide specialist and non-specialist Trainers with idea-generators or models which can be adapted for your own requirements.

Using this section

The programmes are organized by type of training event into:

- general seminars and workshops

- management seminars and workshops

Once you have identified the type of event you need to put on (see design checklist on page 11) turn to the appropriate pages of this section for ideas.
   Remember you will need to adjust the length and content of your programme depending on:

- resources available to you

- training/learning objectives

- target group

General seminars and workshops

Her Majesty's Stationery Office

Management of Stress programme (1 day)

General

1. The identification of stress and its effects, including the distinction between the negative effects of 'stress' and the positive effects of 'pressure'

2. The responses to stress:

- Physiological effects
  - the bodily changes involved in the 'emergency response'

  - the ways in which hormones control mobilisation of energy

- Emotional effects (eg anxiety, frustration, low self-esteem)

- Behavioural and cognitive effects (eg excess drinking, lack of concentration, nervous laughter)

- Health effects (eg headaches, insomnia, psychosomatic disorders)

The individual

3. What do we personally find stressful, both in and out of the workplace?

Stress at work

4. Identification of factors that can be sources of stress at work (eg relationships with others, intrinsic to job, organization versus the family, lack of resources).

The manager

5. The recognition of the results of stress in staff. The responsibility for the wellbeing of staff. The responsibility for the organization of work and resources to prevent as well as manage the problem.

Coping with stress

6. Learn to handle stress by such things as 'Know thyself' questionnaires, clarify objectives, recognize your stress symptoms, develop coping strategies, organize support systems etc.

Counselling staff

7. A look at strategies for helping people, from advice-giving to counselling. The difference between reliance on the expertise of the helper to developing the resources of the 'client'.

8. Case studies are provided whereby syndicate groups role-play a manager and member of staff with a stress problem.

Plenary session

9. Discussion of the day's events, questions etc.

The session on the management course is useful in raising awareness and giving direction to those who wish to pursue the matter further. It has to be said that at times the session can be potentially frustrating (stressful!) if the means of a solution to some of the problems identified are not available.

City Relaxation Counselling

Stress and stress management (10 sessions)

Session 1. Introduction. Explanation of course objectives. What is stress? Personal checklist of symptoms. Contributory factors to hypertension and heart disease.

Demonstration of correct posture and breathing exercises.

Discussion session.

Participation in deep relaxation technique aided by special lighting and music tapes specifically composed for use in relaxation sessions.

Session 2. Stress in the city. The effects on our bodies of crowding, commuting, clockwatching and the office environment.

Sources of work stress.

The Type 'A' personality.

Discussion.

Participation in deep relaxation technique (as above).

Session 3. Smoking, alcohol and drug addiction. Explanation of the physical and mental problems brought about by the above, together with strategies for dealing with these habits. Fact sheets given on each addiction, together with address lists for further information.

Discussion.

Participation in deep relaxation technique.

Session 4. Diet and exercise. Explanation of the health risks brought about by obesity. Distribution of weight charts and weighing of individual group members. Handout sheet on healthy eating. Explanation of why we need to exercise regularly. Handout sheet on healthy exercise.

Demonstration of easy stretching exercises.

Discussion.

Participation in deep relaxation technique.

Session 5. Business travel. The effects of travel on our bodies. Comparison of travelling by road, rail or air. Travel within the UK and Europe and international travel. Effects of worldwide travel against time. The effects of travel on the family of the business executive. Tips on how to travel comfortably by air and how to calculate number of rest days needed to overcome jet-lag.

Discussion.

Participation in deep relaxation technique.

Session 6. Effects of stress on work performance. Explanation of how deep relaxation technique counteracts stress, together with demonstration of biofeedback technology. Distribution of factsheets on relaxation and biofeedback.

Discussion.

Participation in deep relaxation technique with group members using biofeedback equipment.

Session 7. Family stresses. Effects of absence of spouse due to business commitments on family relationships. How change can affect us – explanation of the Life Events Inventory.

Discussion.

Participation in deep relaxation technique with group members using biofeedback equipment.

Session 8. Mid-life crisis. Redundancy, retirement, mid-life crisis, myth or fact? Guidelines for coping with redundancy and/or change to second career. Planning for retirement – is it necessary? Factsheet on how to enjoy your retirement. Useful address list for those about to retire.

Discussion.

Participation in deep relaxation technique with group members using biofeedback equipment.

Session 9. Stress and the woman executive. Profile of the average female manager. Sources of stress on female managers and symptoms of strain. Comparison between stress experienced by female managers and that experienced by male colleagues. What can organizations do to help the female manager of the future? How can the female manager help herself cope with stress?

Discussion – CRC review sheets distributed.

Participation in deep relaxation technique with group members using biofeedback equipment.

Session 10. The importance of leisure, humour and pets in combatting stress.

CRC review sheets collected.

Final discussion.

Final session in deep relaxation technique with group members using biofeedback equipment.

Stress Foundation

A typical programme would include:

1. *Structuring-out role ambiguities.* Expectations by the individual and of others need to be clarified, discussed and readjusted. This requires a process for handling stress resulting from role conflicts as well as ambiguities. Job descriptions are simply insufficient.

2. *Supporting and rewarding tolerance for ambiguity.* The system is in itself ambiguous (ill-defined boundaries, a turbulent environment, unclear objectives, largely immeasurable outputs) and in the end it survives by its responsiveness to internal and external needs. High level creativity and responsiveness go hand in hand with high levels of tolerance. Explaining, learning, coaching, are essential components.

3. *Protecting individual autonomy and initiative.* This follows from the previous point. Teaching/learning systems require professional, mutual accountability, authority with responsibility, delegation, and supporting professional judgements (if judgements are unsound, then they must still be supported, but used as a learning situation for future activities).

4. *'In situ' recovery systems.* Individuals need support systems to be established, and managers will need to have ready immediate sub-systems for dealing with breakdowns in the process system. They must not be *ad hoc.*

5. *Professional referall systems.* Counselling and support services, of the kind provided for students, should be available for staff.

6. *Stressless communications.* The ambiguous, threatening memo, or an overload of crucial information, directives, etc, create more stress than is generally accepted. There is no need for communication to be a stressful process, yet many managers cannot communicate unless it is aggressive, demanding or insensitive, reflecting an aspect of their own perceptions about people and work.

7. *Power equalisation.* Organizations, or the various parts of them, often engage themselves in struggles leading to I win/you

lose, or, I lose/you lose, whereas the less stressful sharing of power to a common agreed end is the I win/you win situation.

8. *Participation.* This must be genuine, or it creates probably the most stress within an organization. Team work, group problem solving, quality circles, team teaching, sharing decisions which affect individuals, are conducive to reducing stress caused by 'them'.

9. *Catharsis sessions.* When things go wrong, there is a need to talk the issues out. Students on a course will usually force at some time a catharsis session in which they express, and hence acknowledge and own, dissatisfaction or feelings of failure, anger etc. In the same way staff have a legitimate need to release their tensions by similar expressions. A wise manager notes and listens to these feelings.

10. *Softening the impact of change.* Warning, discussing, preparing, giving information, listening to suggestions, securing agreement, shifting to meet subordinates' requirements (as well as those of superiors), are the basic ways in which much of the stress of change can be reduced.

11. *Managing overload.* First, the manager must learn himself how to manage his own overload (others seeing an inability to manage overload are stressed by it). Secondly, the manager's role is to pace the level, amount and pressure of work on others. This requires a monitoring sub-system to ensure work loading is as equitable as possible, and that it is spread appropriately over time.

Management seminars and workshops

Civil Service programmes

1. Civil Service College, Management Studies Directorate provides the following programmes:

(i) *Managing stress in organizations*

This is a one-day course designed for staff at Grade 7 level and above. Its aim is to enable senior staff to become more effective in personal and organizational stress management.

Content. This workshop gives participants an opportunity to:

- review their understanding of what stress is, in the light of relevant concepts and examples

- explore how stress can improve as well as impair both personal effectiveness as manager and leader and the performance of organizations, especially in relation to change

- identify stresses and strains in people, systems and structures and develop strategies for managing them

Course content enquiries to: John Henstridge
0990 23444
ext 4232
GTN 2803 4232

The question of 'stress' is covered in the following courses to a greater or lesser extent:

(ii) *Introduction to management for senior staff*

Designed for	Staff at Grades 5–7 level who are relatively inexperienced in management and with little or no previous management training, and senior specialists and professionals for whom management is a relatively small but important, or growing part of their work. It is expected that nominees will have at least some staff to manage though this will not be the only focus of the training.
Aim	To introduce concepts and approaches relevant to effective management.

Course content enquiries
to: Jenny Topham
01–834 6644 ext 3445
GTN 2803 3445

(iii) *Staff management and organization*

Designed for	Staff at Grades 5–7 level who have some previous management training and/or significant management responsibilities.
Aim	To provide a framework within which Civil Service managers can develop their personal competence, together with a practical understanding of their work in its organizational context.

Course content enquiries
to: Julian Rizzello
0990 23444 ext 4347
GTN 2803 4347

(iv) *Senior management course*

Designed for	Staff at Grades 4–5 level who currently have staff to manage and who have some previous management training and experience.

Aim	To give senior managers the opportunity to review their effectiveness against a framework of general competencies in the light of the needs of their current work and to give signposts for further development.

Course content enquiries
to: John Henstridge
0990 23444 ext 4232
GTN 2803 4232

(v) *Senior establishments and personnel course*

Designed for	Staff at Grades 3–5 level in Establishments, Personnel, Organizations and related divisions. The course complements the 'Senior finance courses' and 'Senior management course'.
Aim	To develop a practical and strategic understanding of the role and the function of personnel management in the Civil Service.

Course content enquiries
to: Edward Porter-Hodges
01–834 6644 ext 3344
GTN 2803 3344

2. Civil Service College, Training Resources Group provides training programmes for Training Managers and Trainers. The Training Managers have the opportunity to attend a one-day workshop held at the London Centre, Belgrave Road. Trainers who want to hear more about the topic of stress, or need to develop sessions in this area are encouraged to attend a two and a half day residential course held at Sunningdale. This workshop provides an opportunity for Trainers to examine the topic and to make plans for including some awareness of the topic in their own courses.

The courses are run several times a year on both locations and further details can be obtained from:

Janet Waters
The Civil Service College
Training Resources Group
Sunningdale Park
Ascot
Berks SL5 O6E
Tel. 23444 ext 0990 4324

Ministry of Defence

Three-day workshop for managers

Day One	Day Two	Day Three

Welcome, introductions
 	
Aims, objectives and style of workshop
 	
Syndicate exercise:
 	
    Why are you here?
 	
    Any concerns about the workshop?
	Exercises: breathing and energizing
	
	Assertiveness: a way of avoiding becoming stressed
		Exercises: breathing and energizing
		
		Workshop review: individual group

Syndicate exercise: identify stressors and their effects Categorization of stressors		Pairs exercise: 'dyadic sharing' Plenary review/discussion
Lunch		
Some physiological effects of stress Breathing exercises	Exercise: paint your stress Plenary discussion	Action planning and contracting for the future: individuals and groups
Film: 'Managing stress' Discussion Body relaxation exercises	Further coping strategies for managers Body relaxation exercises	Close

Industrial Society (Pepperell Unit)

Divided loyalties

A one-day workshop about balancing professional and personal responsibilities for:

- equal opportunity, personnel, employee relations, human resource and Line Managers; all who have responsibility for helping individuals in organizations to be as effective as possible

- individual men and women; couples who are concerned about the professional/personal balance issue and the quality of both their work and home life

The aims of the workshop are:

- to help organizations and individuals identify and review the issues involved in managing careers while continuing to manage families and household responsibilities

- to discuss and plan practical and innovative ways of helping other people and ourselves manage more effectively the professional/ personal balancing act; to minimize the stress and use the experience of others.

PROGRAMME

09.15 Registration.

09.30 Welcome and introduction.

09.45 *Work and family life*
A look at the changing work and family patterns in Britain today.

10.15 *Tipping the balance*
What are the things that make getting the right balance so difficult?

A syndicate discussion and report-back.

11.15 *Must success cost so much?*
Organizations and individuals are paying a heavy price by not acknowledging the consequences of work/family pressures or attempting to resolve the divided loyalty conflicts and dilemmas.

- *The skills shortage*
An equal opportunities employer describes why the divided loyalties issue is increasingly one that needs addressing and managing.

- *The stress factor*
A company counsellor talks about the effects stress has on managers, their families and their work performance, and outlines the role played by education, training and counselling.

- *Effective employee and caring parent*
Combining a career with managing a family and household is extremely demanding and requires not only energy and determination but a wide range of organizational skills. Although roles are changing and men and women both know about the strains and gains, it is still women who bear the main responsibility for childcare or the care of elderly or sick relatives. A working mother describes how she manages.

12.45 Lunch

13.30 *Finding a balance*
Sorting priorities, managing time and building support systems. How do we go about it?
A practical exercise.

14.15 *Building in support*
No-one who has career and family responsibilities can be really effective and remain healthy unless they are well-supported both at home and at work. What does this mean in practice? Who has responsibility for what?
Group discussion.

15.00 Tea

15.15 *Building in flexibility*
As family needs become more recognized by employees and employers so too does the case for building more flexible work practices. This session will review some of these practices.

16.00 *Balancing professional and personal responsibilities: making it happen*
An action planning session.
Group discussion and report back.

16.45 Action review.

17.00 Workshop closes.

Industrial Society (Pepperell Unit)

Stress management and counselling skills for managers (2 days)

Day 1. Managing the pressures

09.00 Registration.

09.30 Welcome, introduction and objectives for Day One.

10.00 *What is stress and how does it affect us?*
We all react differently to pressure – sometimes we thrive on it, sometimes we wilt under it. We need to recognize what happens to us and those around us.

11.15 *What are the pressures?*
This session will help participants identify the sources of stress – theirs and other people's.

12.30 Lunch

13.15 *Managing stress*
What can we do to turn negative stress into positive energy?
A review of some practical stress management techniques. Focussing on the importance of leading by example, this session will highlight ways in which we can help our team manage their pressures more effectively.

15.00 *Managing our time*
So often it is constant deadlines and trying to make our time and energy stretch further that puts us under so much uncomfortable pressure. This session will look at key time-management principles and help participants see how they can make more effective use of their own and other people's time.

16.00 *Managing ourselves and other people*
By far our most precious resource as managers, and often the most stressful and difficult one to manage well, is the people for whom we are responsible.

16.45 Action review and summary of the day.

17.00 Workshop ends for the day.

Day Two. Developing our counselling skills

09.00 Introduction and objectives for Day Two.

09.40 *The manager's role as a counsellor*
As managers we are often in situations where good counselling skills are called for: this session will identify different counselling situations, define counselling and the skills we need to develop.

10.30 *Counselling skills 1*
Setting the scene – the practical and logistical issues.
The communication process – how we communicate as counsellors is vital: verbal, non-verbal, listening, feedback.

12.30 Lunch

13.15 *Counselling skills 2*
A look at further counselling techniques, including an introduction to co-counselling.

15.00 *Using a professional*
Sometimes the problems need professional help. This session will look at how and when to refer. A company case study.

16.00 *Making it work*
An action planning session. Both in groups and as individuals, participants will draw together the significant points of the course, make realistic plans to help them manage their own and other people's stress more effectively and see when and how they can apply and develop their counselling skills back at work.

17.00 Workshop ends.

Industrial Society (Pepperell Unit)

Managing the pressures – a stress and time management workshop (1 day)

09.15 Registration.

09.30 Welcome and introduction.

10.00 *What is stress and how does it affect us?*
We all react differently to pressure – sometimes we thrive on it, sometimes we wilt under it. We need to recognize what happens to us and those around us.

11.15 *What are the pressures?*
This session will help participants identify the sources of stress – theirs and other people's.

12.30 Lunch

13.15 *Managing stress*
What can we do to turn negative stress into positive energy? A review of some practical stress management techniques. Focussing on the importance of leading by example, this session will highlight ways in which we can help our team manage their pressures more effectively.

15.00 *Managing our time*
So often it is constant deadlines and trying to make our time and energy stretch further that puts us under so much uncomfortable pressure. This session will look at key time-management principles and help participants see how they can make more effective use of time.

16.00 *Managing ourselves and other people*
By far our most precious resource as managers, and often the most stressful and difficult one to manage well, is the people for whom we are responsible. This final syndicate session will concentrate on practical ways of doing this.

16.45 Action review and summary of the day.

17.00 Workshop ends.

Local Health Authority

Three-day workshop

The workshop is designed for senior managers employed by the Health Authority. The workshop is intensive and largely practical in nature. Teaching methods include formal lectures, small and large discussion groups, an extensive range of handouts, audio tape recordings, psychometric assessment with individual feedback, practical exercises, etc. It is a condition of attendance that strict confidentiality will be maintained by all parties involved in the workshop.

Objectives

The workshop objectives are designed to help participants to:

- identify stressors in their workplace

- gain insight into the many ways (psychophysiological, cognitive and behavioural) in which stress can affect the individual
- recognise stress in those for whom they have a managerial responsibility
- differentiate between assertive, non-assertive and aggressive behaviours and to examine the stress factors related to two of these behaviours
- gain understanding, through the use of psychometric assessment procedures, into their own levels of stress, predisposition to Type 'A' behavioural patterns, irrational belief systems and lack of assertiveness which may contribute to stress
- study a number of models of stress
- receive instruction in a range of skills (cognitive, behavioural, physical) to cope with the effects of stress
- receive individual feedback on the psychometric assessment procedures
- embark on a series of homework exercises in order to generalize, maintain and develop effective ways of coping with stress
- evaluate the effectiveness of the stress management techniques and to assess whether the objectives of the workshop have been maintained

Day One

08.50 Registration.

09.00 Rationale for the workshop.
The learning cycle.
The two stress cycles.

09.30 Introduction to workplace stressors.
Identification of workplace stressors (individual exercise).
Plenary session.

10.45 Morning coffee

11.00 The effects of stress on the individual and the organization.

11.30 Small group exercises.
Plenary session.

12.30 Lunch

13.30 Psychometric assessment.
The Beech questionnaire.
The assertion inventory.
Type 'A' questionnaire.

14.15 *Stress management – health-promoting life styles*
The assertive philosophy – 1.
Assertive, non-assertive and aggressive behaviours.

14.45 Discrimination assessment.
Discussion of results.

Completion of 'Selected items' questionnaire.

15.30 Afternoon tea

15.50 Models of assertion.

16.10 *Stress management – health-promoting life styles*
Progressive relaxation training – 1.
Benefits of deep relaxation.
Initial relaxation training programme (practical exercise).

17.00 End of Day One.

Day Two

08.50 Registration.

09.00 *Stress management – health-promoting life styles*
Principles of rational emotive therapy.
Individual exercise.
Plenary session.

10.00 *Stress management – health-promoting life styles*
The assertive philosophy – 2.
Types of assertive behaviour.
The assertive management of aggression.

11.00 Morning coffee

11.15 Type 'A' behavioural patterns.

11.30 *Stress management – health-promoting life styles*
The management of workplace stressors and Type 'A' behaviours – 1 (small group exercises).

12.30 Lunch

13.30 *Stress management – health-promoting life styles*
The management of workplace stressors and Type 'A' behaviours – 2 (plenary session).

14.30 Stress and the unproductive person.
Characteristics of the unproductive person.
Assertive management.

15.30 Afternoon tea

15.45 Plenary session. Conflict resolution exercise.
Individual feedback of psychometric assessment.

16.15 *Stress management – health-promoting life styles*
Progressive relaxation training – 2.
Intermediate relaxation training programme.
Advanced relaxation training programme.

16.45 *Stress management – health-promoting life styles.*
Time-management principles.

Homework exercises.

17.00 End of Day Two.

Day Three

08.50 Registration.

Morning   The manager as counsellor.
Advanced relaxation training – future
use of the programme.
Generalisation of the progressive
relaxation training.
Discussion of the homework
exercises.

12.30 Lunch

Afternoon   *Stress management – health-
promoting life styles*
Cognitive control methods.
The rights of managers.
Facilitating resolution of conflict.
Resolving conflict (role playing
exercises with video).
Developing an action plan.
Evaluation of workshop.

17.00 End of workshop.

Stress Foundation

In-house course for management (1 day)

This programme, directed principally to senior
management, is an introduction to the whole
field of stress in an organization, and aims to
implant a full understanding of the meaning of
stress, how it is caused, how it is affected by
personality and conditions of employment, and
how it affects the individual and the
organization.
It is preceded by a pre-training self
assessment programme and finally indicates
other sources of help available to the individual.

Module 1
Definition of stress.
Three stages of stress.
Symptoms of stress.
The role of stimulation and challenge.

Module 2
Stressors originating in the work environment.
Manifestations of stress in the employee.
Damage resulting to the organization.
The effect of life changes.
The effect of personality.

Module 3
Stress management in the organization.
Realistic expectations.
Manpower/job fit.
Solving the problems (small group work).

Module 4
Stress management for the individual.
The stress profile.
The symptoms of strain.
Solutions.
Stress control plan.

Training method
The course is fully interactive and numbers are
limited to 12-20 to permit full participation by all.
A folder of course notes, diagrams, and
background information is supplied to each
participant.

Section 3.
Training-resource material

Contents

Introduction

As a Trainer you will be used to researching and developing your own materials for the training topics with which you deal. The subject of stress is no exception to this pattern. This book, however, has been designed to be of practical assistance to you. This section presents certain basic materials which you may find useful.

- sample handouts
- sample overhead projector (OHP) slides
- questionnaires

Further help
Further useful material is available in the book *Understanding Stress – Part One* from which you will be able to:

- adapt subject notes
- group related pages for session notes
- copy illustrations and questionnaires for use with groups

List of films, audio-visual aids etc
Pages 63 to 67 of this book give you details of training aids and materials on stress and related subjects.
Each item is listed to give you information on:

- name and type of training aid
- purpose and training objectives
- supplier's name and address

Using the sample training material

The training material which follows is arranged under the four headings used in *Understanding Stress – Part One.*

- What is stress?
- Symptoms of stress
- Causes of stress
- Managing stress

You will find it most useful to consider the sample material included here in conjunction with *Understanding Stress – Part One.* If you do not have that book available use this sample material in conjunction with the sample programmes on pages 17 to 24 as a basis for developing your own training materials.

Purpose of material
The same training material in this section and Section 1 of *Understanding Stress – Part One* can be used to help you:

- run introductory sessions on stress
- provide an overview for senior management
- devise explanatory sessions for inclusion in general courses

Sources of material
The material which follows comes from a variety of sources and is presented for you to adapt and/or incorporate into your own training events.

What is stress?

A simple definition

An excess of environmental demands over the individual's capacity to meet them.

Stress as a succession of events

- Environmental demands, pressures, forces or stressors on the individual.

- These stressors bring on the stress responses and produce coping mechanisms in the individual.

- The combination of the stress responses and the coping mechanisms lead to physical and mental health or physical and mental illness.

The role of cognition in stress

Objective environmental pressures do not cause predictable stress responses that in their turn cause health or illness. Cognitive processes play a key role in the process. Our perception of the situation is fundamentally important:

- features of our environment only act as stressors if we perceive them as such

- some feature or features of our environment are likely to bring on the stress responses if they are perceived as:

  - unpleasant
  - uncontrollable
  - unpredictable

- our perception of the coping mechanisms available to us and their likely success or failure is also significant.

The role of mediating factors in stress

There are many mediating factors that influence the way in which stressors lead to health or illness.

Some of the most important factors include the health of the organism, its nutritional state, the skills, experience, assets and resources of the individual and the versatility and adequacy of its defences.

Considerable attention has been devoted to the study of the following sets of factors:

- habitual behaviour patterns or personality

- life style

- social support

Social factors have a considerable influence on these mediating factors. The following factors are likely to be particularly important:

- cultural and sub-cultural origins and membership

- social class and socio-economic factors, including income and occupation

- education and training

- age

What is stress?

DEMAND ON INDIVIDUAL

PERCEIVED AS THREAT

FIGHT/FLIGHT REACTION

PHYSIOLOGICAL IMBALANCE

EFFECTS ON PERFORMANCE

What is stress?

A stressful circumstance is one with which you cannot cope successfully, or believe you cannot cope successfully, and which results in unwanted physical, mental or emotional reactions.

What is stress?

The three phases of the General Adaptation Syndrome

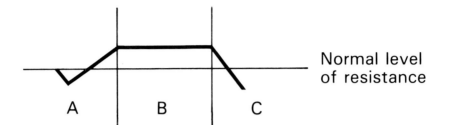

Normal level of resistance

A **Alarm reaction** The body shows the changes characteristic of the first exposure to the stressor. At the same time, its resistance is diminished and, if the stressor is sufficiently strong (severe burns, extremes of temperature), death may result.

B **Stage of resistance** Resistance ensues if continued exposure to the stressor is compatible with adaptation. The bodily signs characteristic of the alarm reaction have virtually disappeared, and resistance ensues.

C **Stage of exhaustion** Following long-continued exposure to the same stressor, to which the body has become adjusted, eventually adaptation energy is exhausted. The signs of alarm reaction reappear, but now they are irreversible, and the individual can suffer permanent damage (even die).

What is stress?

Symptoms of stress at each stage

STAGE I
- Speeding up
- Talking quickly
- Walking fast (head leading)
- Eating and drinking faster
- Working at high speed and for long periods of time without tiring (at the time)

STAGE II
- Irritability
- Dyspepsia and gastric symptoms, eg heartburn
- Tension headache
- Migraine
- Insomnia, loss of energy
- Comfort tricks: alcohol, smoking
- Increased intake of food etc.

STAGE III
- Cotton wool head
- Gastric ulceration
- Palpitations, chest pain, cardiac incident
- Depression and anxiety
- Tiredness, lack of energy
- Physical or mental breakdown

Source: Stress Foundation

SAMPLE HANDOUT

What is stress?

The three stages of the stress response

The response	What happens	The effect
FIGHT OR FLIGHT	Red alert. Body and brain prepare for action, extra energy released.	Response to danger, meet it and return to equilibrium.
SECONDARY	Fats, sugars and cortico steroids released for more energy.	Unless extra fats etc used up then third stage moved into.
EXHAUSTION	Energy stores used up.	Serious illness leading to death.

What is stress?

Human performance and stress

An adaptation of the human performance curve.

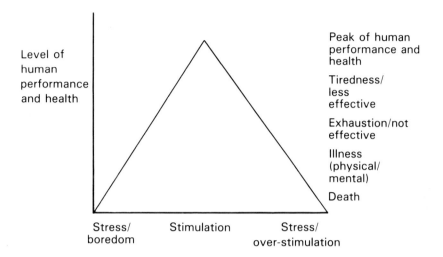

This model highlights lack of challenge as having similar effects to overstimulation, and that these effects can be progressive. It can also be used to raise the point that early recognition of the effects of stress can enable the individual to prevent their progression into ineffectiveness and ill-health.

Source: BOND, M and KILTY, J. *Practical methods of dealing with stress.* Human Potential Research project. University of Surrey. 1982.

What is stress?

Habitual behaviour patterns as a mediating factor

Introduction – Type 'A' and Type 'B' behaviours

Friedman and Rosenman looked into the relationship between people's habitual ways of behaving and their associated risk of heart attacks. They identified high risk behaviours which they called Type 'A' and low risk behaviour which they called Type 'B'. This handout looks at work which has developed from their pioneering work. In general Type 'B' behaviours are the opposite of Type 'A' behaviours.

Type 'A' behaviour patterns

- excessively hard-driving, busy
- ambitious and striving for upward social mobility; wanting more things
- enhanced sense of time urgency, pre-occupation with time deadlines, desire to do increasingly more things in less time, a feeling that time is passing too quickly
- pre-occupation with competitive activities; feeling the challenge of responsibility
- aggressive, hostile and impatient
- a belief that their patterns of behaviour are responsible for their success
- autonomous, dominant and self-confident
- hyperalertness with tense facial musculature and explosive speech stylistics

Explanations of Type 'A' behaviours

There are both social and psychological explanations of Type 'A' behaviours:

1. **Social explanations** locate Type 'A' behaviours within a social context in which the dominant values are towards achievement, upward social mobility, economic growth, scientific advancement and technological development.

*FRIEDMAN, M. D. and ROSENMAN, R. H. *Type 'A' behaviour and your heart*. Wildwood House. 1975. ISBN 0704501589.

2. **Psychological explanations** usually posit some sort of neurotic need that is being satisfied, for example:

- the need to master or control a potentially uncontrollable environment
- a struggle against people, objects in the environment and time
- a lack of a continuous and basic sense of security
- a failure to gauge their intrinsic intellectual and emotional capabilities

Some further characteristics of Type 'A's

Many studies have looked at the characteristics of people who exhibit Type 'A' behaviour patterns in a wide range of different contexts. The following is a summary of some of the findings:

- work longer hours
- spend more time in classes (students)
- travel more for business
- get less sleep
- more involved in voluntary clubs and organizations, community groups etc
- spend less time in relaxation and recreation
- work more around the home
- communicate less with their wives (men)
- less marital sex
- derive little pleasure from socialising

Characteristics of Type 'B' behaviour

Ability to take a long view. Unlike 'A's, Type 'B' people don't try to 'over-egg the pudding.' They don't try to meet unrealistic targets or to take on more than they can cope with. Often they are better at delegating. They don't expect a task to be done *exactly* as they would do it – but they do trust their subordinates to accomplish it.

Speed is not the issue. Type 'B's are not clock-watchers, and are secure enough within themselves not to complete every task to deadline. Whatever they do they give their full attention to it.

Sense of personal identity. They don't feel that they have to earn respect and love, but are secure in who they are and what they do. They take into account not what may be, but what was and what is.

Sense of proportion. The constant struggle and anger of the Type 'A' is wholly foreign to Type 'B's. They always maintain a sense of balance at events in their lives.

The two extremes

Friedman's and Rosenman's work gives some insight into why some people are more prone to stress-related disease. It needs to be emphasized that Type 'A' and Type 'B' behaviour can only be seen as a yardstick – there are no absolutes. Most people will fall somewhere between the two extreme types described.

SAMPLE HANDOUT (CONT'D)

What is stress?

The person/environment fit

Ivancevich and Mattesson have developed a model of the *subjective person/environment fit.** They argue that, in the same way that there are Type 'A' and Type 'B' persons, so there are Type 'A' and Type 'B' work environments. That is to say there are work environments that suit Type 'A's and those that suit Type 'B's. These are described briefly below:

1. *Optimal Type 'A' work environment*

- controllable
- fast-paced
- extremely challenging

2. *Optimal Type 'B' work environment*

- routine
- moderately-paced
- moderately challenging

The interaction model of Type 'A'–'B' person/work environments posits four possible sets of conditions of which two are congruent and two incongruent:

```
                          I    II
              'A'    ┌─────────┬─────────┐
                     │ 'A'–'A' │ 'B'–'A' │
   Work              │congruence│incongruence│
   environment       ├─────────┼─────────┤
                     │ 'A'–'B' │ 'B'–'B' │
              'B'    │incongruence│congruence│
                     │      IV │ III     │
                     └─────────┴─────────┘
                         'A'       'B'
```

Behaviour patterns

1. 'A' behaviour in 'A' environment: good fit

Workers are encouraged to make their own decisions, take initiative and carry more responsibility.

This may become too demanding if the work pace becomes frenetic and unending. Then the workload becomes excessive, a sense of time urgency develops and the individual fails to control the environment.

2. 'B' behaviour in 'A' environment: poor fit

An easy-going, relaxed, thorough and less aggressive person is unsuited to the demands of the environment.

There are likely to be physical, psychological and organizational problems for the individual.

3. 'B' behaviour in 'B' environment: good fit

The easy-going, relaxed person is well suited to the routine, moderately challenging environment.

4. 'A' behaviour in 'B' environment: poor fit

The individual finds the work too routine, too slow and insufficiently challenging.

There are likely to be physical, psychological and organizational problems for the individual.

Reducing Type 'A' behaviours

Individuals who exhibit Type 'A' behaviours are still at considerable risk, even in Type 'A' environments. It is therefore useful to think about reducing Type 'A' behaviours. A holistic approach involving the whole person in all aspects of their life seems most appropriate. This involves:

1. recognizing one's behaviour patterns, understanding their effects and understanding what underlies them.

2. replacing existing beliefs, assumptions and attributes with new and realistic values and goals.

3. restructuring the environment in a range of ways, for example:

- consciously giving up control and risking greater spontaneity
- learning to relax without guilt into creative hobbies and leisure
- focusing more on the quality of one's relationships
- seeking more humour and fun
- learning to become a listener
- doing one thing at a time

*IVANCEVICH, J. M. and MATTESON, M. T. *Stress and work: a managerial perspective.* Scott, Foresman, 1980.

Symptoms of stress

Signs of strain which must be taken seriously

Signs of strain in physical health

- recurrent headaches

- ringing in the ears or frequent head noises

- frequent use of antacids or other self-prescribed drugs.

- palpitations and chest pain

- frequent heartburn, stomach cramps, diarrhoea, being full of gas, unable to swallow

- trembling under any extra pressure, leg cramps or pain, twitching in limbs

- feeling that you may pass out

- getting any illness that is around

Signs of strain in intellectual function

- having frequent thick cotton wool head (without excessive alcohol!)

- loss of former concentration

- loss of former reliable memory

- a new inability to reach satisfactory decisions

- new difficulty in thinking around problems

- new difficulty in dismissing problems from the mind

- insomnia

All are evidence of a tired mind

Signs of strain in emotional health

- a feeling of being very low or dulled

- a shut-down in all emotions except anger and irritation

- all joy, laughter and pleasure have dried up

- active love and caring have lessened or disappeared

- tears seem very near frequently for no reason

All are evidence of exhausted emotional health

Source: Stress Foundation

SAMPLE HANDOUT

Symptoms of stress

How much stress do I have?

Mind
- I have frequent headaches although my doctor says there is nothing wrong with me
- I sometimes hear head noises, ringing or buzzing in the ears
- My memory seems to have gone lately
- I can't stop thinking about one particular thing. It goes round and round in my head
- I can't seem to settle down and get on with things I have to do. I keep putting them off
- I can't concentrate on anything these days
- My head often feels full of cotton wool and I can't think through it

Body
- I often have aches and pains in the back of the neck but my doctor says there is nothing wrong
- My shoulders and back ache at the end of the day – without having had hard physical exercise
- I sometimes have difficulty in keeping my hands from trembling
- I sigh often
- I sometimes feel that I cannot get enough breath in my lungs
- I frequently have cramp in my limbs
- I sometimes feel that I am going to pass out
- I frequently have diarrhoea. I have had tests and they say there is nothing wrong
- Sometimes my rings get very tight and I have difficulty in doing up my skirt or trousers

- I am sometimes very gassy and burp a lot
- Some days I frequently need to go to the lavatory to pass water. I am told there is nothing wrong with me
- I take a long time to go to sleep
- I frequently wake up in the early hours of the morning and have difficulty in getting back to sleep
- I get very hot at night and my heart beat seems louder and faster
- My heart seems to skip beats, but the doctor says it is quite healthy

Social Life
- People at work are very difficult
- There are too many demands on me and too much change
- I have no real friend to confide in
- Life is nothing but work and sleep
- I have family problems and I don't really know anyone

Emotional Life
- I am often very near to tears/I rarely laugh these days
- I react to everything with the same feeling. There aren't any ups or downs now
- The least little thing sets me off
- I feel tense and wound up for much of the time
- I seem to have lost the ability to feel or to care for anything or anyone

Symptoms of stress

Some early warning signs

The following are lists of the common physical, mental, emotional and behavioural symptoms of stress. As personal stress increases more of these symptoms are likely to become apparent. By noticing how many of these items you are currently experiencing, either continuously or from time to time, you can obtain an early warning of an increase in stress. Even though some of the symptoms may have a clear physical cause, count them nevertheless, for their occurrence is still likely to be an indirect consequence of stress.

Physical signs
- headaches
- indigestion
- palpitations – throbbing heart
- breathlessness
- nausea – feeling sick
- muscle twitches
- tiredness
- vague aches or pains
- skin irritation or rashes
- susceptibility to allergies
- excessive sweating
- clenched fists or jaw
- fainting
- frequent colds, flu or other infections
- recurrence of previous illnesses
- constipation or diarrhoea
- rapid weight gain or loss

Mental signs
- indecision
- memory failing
- loss of concentration, easily distracted
- tunnel vision
- bad dreams or nightmares
- worrying
- muddled thinking
- making mistakes
- less intuitive
- less sensitive
- persistent negative thoughts

- impaired judgement
- more short-term thinking
- hasty decisions

Emotional signs
- irritability
- more suspicious
- more gloomy, depressed
- more fussy
- feeling tense
- drained, no enthusiasm
- under attack
- cynical, inappropriate humour
- alienated
- feeling nervous, apprehensive, anxious
- feeling of pointlessness
- loss of confidence
- less satisfaction in life
- demotivated
- reduced self-esteem
- job dissatisfaction

Behavioural signs
- unsociability
- restlessness
- loss of appetite or overeating
- loss of interest in sex, or overuse
- disurbed sleep or insomnia
- drinking more alcohol
- smoking more
- taking work home more
- too busy to relax
- not looking after oneself
- lying
- anti-social behaviour
- unable to unwind
- low productivity
- accident prone
- bad driving
- impaired speech
- voice tremor
- increased problems at home
- poor time management
- withdrawing from supportive relationships

Symptoms of stress

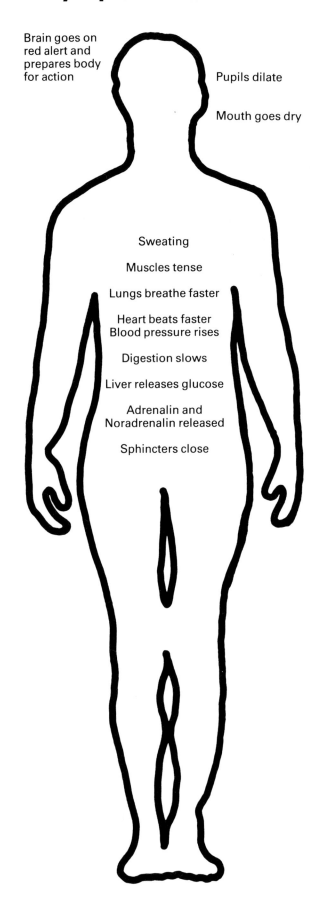

Brain goes on
red alert and
prepares body
for action

Pupils dilate

Mouth goes dry

Sweating

Muscles tense

Lungs breathe faster

Heart beats faster
Blood pressure rises

Digestion slows

Liver releases glucose

Adrenalin and
Noradrenalin released

Sphincters close

Causes of stress

Examples of unrealistic beliefs

1. The idea that it is a dire necessity for an adult human being to be approved by all significant others.

2. The idea that one should be thoroughly competent, adequate and achieving important things if one is to consider oneself worthwhile.

3. The idea that human unhappiness is externally caused and that people have little or no ability to control their sorrows or disturbances.

4. The idea that if something is/may be dangerous or fearsome you should be terribly concerned about it and should keep dwelling on the possibility of its occurring.

5. The idea that it is easier to avoid than to face certain difficult situations in life.

6. The idea that one should be dependent on others and need someone stronger than oneself on whom to rely.

7. The idea that one's past history is an all-important determinant of one's present behaviour, and that because something once strongly affected one's life, it should indefinitely have a similar effect.

8. The idea that one should become quite upset over other people's problems.

9. The idea that there is invariably a right, precise and perfect solution to human problems, and nothing else will do.

Source: Alistair Ostell. Occupational Psychology Management Centre, University of Bradford.

SAMPLE HANDOUT

Causes of stress

Problems of underload and overload

What would you do in the following situations?

1. **Man works late, takes work home every night, is reluctant to take breaks or holidays, staff find him 'difficult'.**

   What is the underlying problem? What do you do?

2. **Man bored, apathetic, uninterested, unmotivated, can't 'get through to him'.**

   What is the underlying problem? What do you do?

3. **Employee always says 'I don't know what I'm supposed to be doing half the time'.**

   What is wrong? Is grouse legitimate?

4. **Atmosphere of suspicion – resistance to innovation and change. Trouble in that section.**

   What do you do?

5. **Higher absenteeism than norm for one area.**

   What do you do?

6. **Employees' holiday leave has to be cancelled in one section.**

   What action do you take as manager?

Source: Stress Foundation

Causes of stress

An overview of potential sources of management stress

1. **Intrinsic to job**
   - too much work
     - qualitative
     - quantitative
   - too little work
   - time pressure/deadlines
   - poor physical working conditions
   - mistakes
   - too many decisions

2. **Role in organization**
   - role ambiguity
   - role conflict
   - too little responsibility
   - no participation in decision-making
   - responsibility for people
   - responsibility for things
   - lack of managerial support
   - increasing standards of acceptable performance
   - organizational boundaries (internal and external)

3. **Relations within organization**
   - poor relations with boss
   - poor relations with colleagues and subordinates
   - difficulties in delegating responsibility
   - personality conflicts

4. **Career development**
   - over-promotion
   - under-promotion
   - lack of job security
   - fear of redundancy/retirement
   - fear of obsolescence
   - thwarted ambition
   - sense of being trapped

5. **Organizational structure and climate**
   - restrictions on behaviour (eg budgets)
   - lack of effective consultation and communication
   - uncertainty about what is happening
   - no sense of belonging
   - loss of identity
   - office politics

6. **Organization interface with outside**
   - divided loyalties (company versus own interests)
   - conflicts with family demands

7. **Intrinsic to individual**
   - personality (tolerance for ambiguity, stable self-concept, etc)
   - inability to cope with change
   - declining abilities
   - lack of insight into own motivation and stress
   - ill-equipped to deal with interpersonal problems
   - fear of moving out of area of expertise

Source: HM Land Registry

SAMPLE HANDOUT

Managing stress

Coping mechanisms

Introduction

There are many different strategies that people use in order to deal with stress. These can be arranged on a scale between two extreme positions of avoidance and constructive action. The main points on such a scale are: avoidance, passivity, palliatives and action.

The sort of categorization described above implies that as one moves from avoidance to action so the coping mechanisms become increasingly effective. This is not, however, necessarily the case. Thus, for example, avoidance may be the most effective mechanism if there is no available course of action that is likely to actually work. Similarly, constructive action may actually be counter-productive if the problem is so large and complex that to try and solve it builds in failure.

The actual choice of coping mechanisms in any set of circumstances will depend on the following sorts of things:

- The appraisal of the stress made by the individual (eg how pleasant/unpleasant it is, how controllable/uncontrollable it is, whether it is in an area of life that is of central importance or not).

- The characteristics of the individual (eg Type 'A'/Type 'B', orientation to work, skills, experience, assets, resources).

- The characteristics of the environment in which the problem arises (eg size of the organization, network of social roles in which the problem emerged).

Coping mechanisms

Avoidance ie avoiding acknowledging, confronting or dealing with the problem in an action-oriented manner. The extreme form of this would be repression, where we deny the problem to ourselves and keep it at a subconscious level. A less extreme form would be supression, where we do not actually deny it to ourselves but we actively push it out of our mind. A less extreme form still would be denial where we deny it to others. Other forms of avoidance include withdrawal from the source of the problem and actively avoid dealing with the problem.

Passivity ie being passive in our response to the situation. This may involve doing nothing, doing what we are told, accepting the status quo without trying to change things etc.

Palliatives ie attempting to alleviate the problem without actually curing it. Some palliatives are likely to be counter-productive in the longer term (eg increased smoking, drinking and other drug use) as well as more passive palliatives (eg staying at home and watching television). Other palliatives may help us to bounce back (eg domestic activity, active leisure, personal development) and the development of a healthy life style (eg exercises, relaxation techniques). It is, however, important to recognise that even healthy palliatives may be counter-productive (eg sports injuries arising from over-exercise).

Action ie doing something about the problem itself either at an emotional level (eg acknowledging, expressing and dealing with feelings) or a substantive level (eg acknowledging, confronting and dealing with problems). It may be useful to think of both who one does this with and how one does it:

- Problems can be dealt with alone or with other people. There are very real advantages in 'getting away' from people and having some 'privacy' but the cost is the lack of social and emotional support as well as the loss of an alternative viewpoint. Possible people to talk to include one's partner, peers and friends, specialists and experts and the people involved in the problem. These may vary in many ways including their closeness to the issue and the degree of risk or threat.

- The approach to problem-solving specified in most textbooks involves the following sequence of events: collect information, identify problems, identify alternative solutions, evaluate alternative solutions, prepare action plans, implement and review.

Source: Stress Foundation

Managing stress

Understanding and control of stress

1. **Understanding the human stress response**

   Its function: • to give more energy as and when required

   Its use: • to help to meet deadlines and crises easily and calmly

   Its dangers: • interference with entire function if kept on for too long and at too high a level

2. **Understanding that strain is largely derived from a mis-match between the individual and demanding situations in life**

   Combat by: • mastery of the job through training
   • development of self-esteem through involvement and control
   • resolution of conflict through action and communication
   • knowing when to seek medical or counselling help
   • group support

3. **Control of over-arousal**

   Through: • knowledge of reactions to difficult situations
   • knowledge of potential stressors in environment
   • learning how to maximise efficiency and effective function through daily unstressing techniques
   • knowing personal energy patterns and working with them

Source: Stress Foundation

45

Managing stress

Life style as a mediating factor

Introduction

Our life styles influence the effect that stress has. Below is a list of some of the facets of our life style that may be important.

Diet

- avoid saturated fats, sugar and salt
- eat plenty of fibre
- eat plenty of fresh fruit and vegetables, especially raw ones
- avoid processed foods

If you smoke, drink or consume a lot of tea or coffee or are under a lot of stress then consider supplements of vitamins B and C and zinc.

Drugs

- avoid all drugs including tobacco, alcohol (apart from occasional, moderate social use), tranquillisers and sleeping pills

Exercise

- take a brisk walk of at least two miles several times a week
- participate in non-competitive aerobic exercise (preferably something like swimming or cycling) for a period of 15 minutes or more at least twice a week

Environment

- avoid living in or working in urban centres with heavy traffic
- avoid water supplied through lead pipes in a soft water area
- maintain high standards of domestic and personal cleanliness
- keep the house clean and ensure that your hands are clean before you eat or prepare food
- wash all fresh fruit and vegetables before use
- Avoid working with dangerous chemicals, especially neurotoxins such as lead, mercury, carbon monoxide, manganese, toluene, and trichlorethylene

Rest, relaxation and leisure

- allow yourself time to relax and unwind at the end of a busy day and at the end of a busy week
- allow yourself the time to do the things that you find relaxing, whatever they may be
- allow yourself time to have the sleep that you need
- partake in interests and leisure activities outside of work
- engage in some technique of relaxation (eg meditation, autogenics, yoga)
- avoid stressful activities like driving, flying etc
- allow plenty of time to eat, and eat leisurely

Managing stress

Social support as a mediating factor

Introduction

Social support is an important factor in reducing the effects of stress. It is not, however, sufficient merely to be a part of an extensive range of social networks. What is particularly important is having:

- intimate, confiding relationships in which there is an exchange of intimate information

- the presence of social solidarity or cohesion in relationships ie feeling a part of the family, the group, the company or whatever

Sources of social support

There are many possible sources of social support including the following:

- one's partner
- family
- friends
- work group
- wider social contacts at work

- social contacts through leisure, interests etc
- professional or specialist contacts including one's doctor, welfare or whatever

Social marginality

The problems of social isolation and living alone are well-known and well-documented. Less well-known are the problems of 'social marginality' and people who are members of minority groups. These individuals tend to be more vulnerable to the adverse effects of stress in their lives. This appears to be true for members of all sorts of minority groups.

Status inconsistency

'Status inconsistency' is another social factor that appears to reduce people's capacity to deal with stress effectively. Status inconsistency arises when there is a lack of fit between different aspects of our social status (eg education, occupation, income, housing). An example would be someone from a poor working class background living in an affluent middle class area.

SAMPLE HANDOUT

Managing stress

Coping checklist

To what extent does each of the following fit as a description of you? (Circle one number on each line across.)

	Very true	Quite true	Some- what true	Not very true	Not at all true
1. I roll with the punches when problems come up	1	2	3	4	5
2. I spend almost all my time thinking about my work	5	4	3	2	1
3. I treat other people as individuals and care about their feelings and opinions	1	2	3	4	5
4. I recognise and accept my own limitations and assets	1	2	3	4	5
5. There are quite a few people I could describe as 'good friends'	1	2	3	4	5
6. I enjoy using my skills and abilities both on and off the job	1	2	3	4	5
7. I get bored easily	5	4	3	2	1
8. I enjoy meeting and talking with people who have different ways of thinking about the world	1	2	3	4	5
9. Often in my job I 'bite off more than I can chew'	5	4	3	2	1
10. I'm usually very active at weekends with recreation or projects	1	2	3	4	5
11. I prefer working with people who are very much like myself	5	4	3	2	1
12. I work mainly because I have to live and not necessarily because I enjoy what I do	5	4	3	2	1
13. I believe I have a realistic picture of my strengths and weaknesses	1	2	3	4	5
14. I often get into arguments with people who don't think my way	5	4	3	2	1
15. I often have trouble getting much done on my job	5	4	3	2	1
16. I'm interested in a lot of different topics	1	2	3	4	5
17. I get upset when things don't go my way	5	4	3	2	1
18. Often I'm not sure where I stand on a controversial topic	5	4	3	2	1
19. I'm usually able to find a way around anything which stops me from an important goal	1	2	3	4	5
20. I often disagree with my boss or others at work	5	4	3	2	1

Managing stress

Context checklist

How do you feel about each of the following in your job? (Circle one number in each line across.)

	Very satis- fied	Satis- fied	Neu- tral	Dis- satis- fied	Very dis- satis- fied
1. How satisfied are you with the section you work in compared with other sections, divisions etc you know about?	1	2	3	4	5
2. How satisfied are you with your job – the kind of work you do?	1	2	3	4	5
3. How satisfied are you with your physical working conditions (heat, light, noise etc)?	1	2	3	4	5
4. How satisfied are you with the extent to which people you work with co-operate well with one another?	1	2	3	4	5
5. How satisfied are you with the job your immediate boss is doing in managing his/her responsibilities for people?	1	2	3	4	5
6. How satisfied are you with the job your immediate boss is doing in managing his/her task responsibilities?	1	2	3	4	5
7. How satisfied are you with your pay considering your duties and responsibilities?	1	2	3	4	5
8. How satisfied are you with your pay considering what non-Civil Service organizations pay for similar types of work?	1	2	3	4	5
9. How satisfied are you with your advancement to better jobs since you started to work in this organization?	1	2	3	4	5
10. How satisfied are you with your opportunities to move into a better job in the department?	1	2	3	4	5
11. How satisfied are you with the extent to which your present job makes full use of your skills and abilities?	1	2	3	4	5
12. How satisfied are you with the level of mental ability requirements of your present job (problem solving, judgement, technical knowledge etc)?	1	2	3	4	5
13. How satisfied are you with the hours worked in your present job?	1	2	3	4	5
14. Now considering everything how would you rate your overall feelings about your employment situation at the present time?	1	2	3	4	5

15. If you have your way will you be working for the same organization five years from now?

    Circle one:

    1. Certainly   4. Probably not

    2. Probably   5. Certainly not

    3. I'm not at all sure   6. I'll be retired in five years

Managing stress

Stress checklist – work factors

Listed below are various kinds of problems that may arise in your work. Indicate to what extent you find each of them to be a problem, concern or obstacle in carrying out your job duties and responsibilities.

This factor is a problem....	Never	Sel-dom	Some-times	Usu-ally	Always
Conflict and uncertainty					
1. Not knowing just what the people you work with expect of you	1	2	3	4	5
2. Feeling that you have to do things on the job that are against your better judgement	1	2	3	4	5
3. Thinking that you will not be able to satisfy the conflicting demands of various people over you	1	2	3	4	5
Job pressure					
4. Feeling that you have too heavy a workload; one that you can't possibly finish during an ordinary day	1	2	3	4	5
5. Not having enough time to do the work properly	1	2	3	4	5
6. Having the requirements of the job conflict/impose upon your personal life	1	2	3	4	5
Job scope					
7. Being unclear about just what the scope and responsibilities of your job are	1	2	3	4	5
8. Feeling that you have too little authority to carry out the responsibilities assigned to you	1	2	3	4	5
9. Not being able to get the information you need to carry out your job	1	2	3	4	5
Rapport with management					
10. Not knowing what your manager or supervisor thinks of you – how he or she evaluates your performance	1	2	3	4	5
11. Not being able to predict the reactions of people above you	1	2	3	4	5
12. Having ideas considerably different from those of your managers	1	2	3	4	5

Managing stress

Scoring directions

Page 48 – Coping checklist

Add together the numbers you circled for the four questions in each of the coping scales (see below for the appropriate questions).

Coping scale	Add together the answers to these questions	Your score (write in)
Knows self	4, 9, 13, 18	_____
Many interests	2, 5, 7, 16	_____
Variety of reactions	1, 11, 17, 19	_____
Accepts other values	3, 8, 14, 20	_____
Active and productive	6, 10, 12, 15	_____

Add the five scores together for the total score _____

Scores for each area can vary between 5 and 20. Scores of 12 or more suggest it may be useful to direct more attention to that area.
   The overall score can range between 20 and 100.
Scores of 60 or more may suggest some general difficulty in coping with the areas covered.

Page 49 – Context checklist

Add together the numbers you circled and enter the total here _____

Scores on this survey range between 14 and 75. Scores of 45 or more may suggest the overall context of your work is less than satisfactory. You should also look at the specific items you rated negatively.

Page 50 – Stress checklist

Add together the three numbers you circled within each of the four areas and enter them here:

Conflict and uncertainty _____

Job pressure _____

Job scope _____

Rapport with management _____

Then add them all together for overall score _____

Scores on each of the four areas can range between 3 and 15.
Scores of 9 and above may suggest that the area may be presenting a problem which warrants your attention.
   The overall total score can range between 12 and 60. Scores of 36 or more may suggest a more than desirable amount of stress in your job environment.

Source: McLean, A. A. *Work stress.* Addison Wesley. 1979.

51

Section 4.
Further sources of help

Contents

Introduction

List of organizations/individuals
This book cannot deal exhaustively with the subject of stress but for your information this section contains details of organizations and individuals who can provide further help and information.

The list is divided by broad subject areas (see below). Each entry gives name, address and, where possible, telephone number and a brief indication of what the organization does.

Training materials and aids
The information given includes the type, title/description of the material, its purpose/training objectives and name of supplier, with address and telephone number where possible.

Courses
Prices where quoted were correct at time of going to press, but should always be checked, as they are liable to change.

List of organizations/individuals

Age

Age Concern

Bernard Sunley House
60 Pitcairns Road
Mitcham
Surrey CR4 3LL

01–640 5431

Advice and information for the elderly and those who care for them.

Alcohol

ACCEPT

20 Seagrave Road
London SW6 1RQ

01–381 3155

Counselling, therapy and relaxation training for problem drinkers.

Alcohol Counselling Service

34 Electric Lane
London SW9 8JT

01–737 3579

Provides a direct counselling service.

Alcoholics Anonymous

PO Box 514
11 Redcliffe Gardens
London SW10 9BQ

01–352 9779

2,000 mutual support groups for problem drinkers.

Aquarius

4 St George's Street
Northampton NN1 2TN

0604 32421

Counselling for problem drinkers and their families.

Anorexia

Anorexic Aid

The Priory Centre
11 Priory Road
High Wycombe
Bucks HP13 6SL

0494 21431

A network of self-help groups for anorexics or bulimiacs.

Bereavement

The Compassionate Friends

6 Denmark Street
Bristol BS1 5DQ

0272 292778

Help for bereaved parents.

Cruse

Cruse House
126 Sheen Road
Richmond
Surrey TW9 1UR

01–940 4818/9047

Organization for widows and their children.

Complementary medicine

British Chiropractic Association

Information Service
5 First Avenue
Chelmsford
Essex CM1 1RX

0245 358487

Provides list of practitioners.

British Homeopathic Association

27A Devonshire Street
London W1N 1RJ

01–935 2163

Provides list of homeopathic practitioners.

British Hypnotherapy Association

67 Upper Berkeley Square
London W1H 7DH

01–723 4443

Provides detailed information, including names of practitioners.

Institute of Complementary Medicine

21 Portland Place
London W1N 3AF

01–636 9543

Information and advice on all aspects of complementary medicine.

Joint Development Resources

24 Cecil Park
Pinner
Middlesex HA5 5HH

01–866 1262

Publications and teaching to control stress, using the Alexander technique.

Osteopaths General Council and Register Ltd

1 Suffolk Street
London SW1Y 4HG

01–839 2060

Provides a list of registered osteopaths (MRO).

Society of Teachers of the Alexander Technique

10 London House
226 Fulham Road
London SW10 9EL

01–351 0828

Provides a list of teachers of the Alexander method (a technique to reduce muscle tension).

Counselling

British Association for Counselling

37A Sheep Street
Rugby
Warwickshire CV21 3BX

0788 78328

Information, advice and publications.

Managers' Counselling Association

Sundridge Park Management College
Plaistow Road
Bromley
Kent BR1 3TP

01–460 8585/8987

Counselling for managers.

Isis Centre

Little Clarendon Street
Oxford OX1 2HS

0865 56648

NHS counselling service.

Samaritans

See local telephone directory.

Tavistock Clinic

120 Belsize Lane
London NW3 5BA

01–435 7111

Self-referral counselling service for young people aged 16–30. NHS funded.

Depression

Depressives Anonymous

36 Chestnut Avenue
Beverley
North Humberside HU17 9QU

0482 860619

Mutual-help organization, working with medical service.

Depressives Associated

PO Box 5
Castletown
Portland
Dorset DT5 1BQ

Mutual help organization which believes the medical services do not understand depression.

Drugs

ASH

Margaret Pyke House
23–35 Mortimer Street
London W1N 7RJ

01–637 9843

Action on smoking and health.

Families Anonymous

88 Caledonian Road
London N1 9DN

01–227 8805

Self-help for relatives and friends of drug users.

National Tranquiliser Advisory Council (TRANX)

17 Peel Road
Harrow
Middlesex HA3 7QX

01–427 2065

Telephone and personal counselling, and group support.

Health

British Holistic Medical Association

179 Gloucester Place
London NW1 6DX

01–262 5299

Conferences, workshops, lectures and publications.

City Health Care

4–7 Chiswell Street
London EC1Y 4TH

01–638 4988

Established in early 1986, this organization
provides a stress management counselling
service and guidance on preventative health
care. Individual consultation, workshops and
seminars are arranged.

College of Health

19 Victoria Park Square
London E2 9PF

01–980 6263

Publishes *Self Health,* a magazine on physical
and mental health. Members can ask the college
for advice and information.

Devonshire Clinic

21 Devonshire Place
London W1N 1PD

01–935 2565

Integrated health assessments including
medical, psychosocial, physiotherapy and
occupational assessment to provide a thorough
check-up on the health of the whole person.
Accepts clients from organizations and
individuals.

Institute of Occupational Medicine

8 Roxburgh Place
Edinburgh EH8 9SU

031–667 5131

Multi-disciplinary research into the work
environment and health. Contact the librarian for
further information.

St Andrew's Hospital

Billing Road
Northampton NN1 5DG

0604 29696

Treatment for stress disorders, including anxiety
management, relaxation, social skills training
and problem solving.

Women's Health Information Centre

52 Featherstone Street
London EC17 8RT

01–251 6580

Information on women's health and self-help
groups.

Health and Safety at Work

British Occupational Hygiene Society

1 St Andrew's Place
Regents Park
London NW1 4LB

01–486 4860

Holds conferences and workshops to discuss
problems with specific industries and with
specific stressors.

Health and Safety Executive

Library and Information Services
Broad Lane
Sheffield S3 7HQ

0742 752539

Information on organizations, regulations etc.

Loneliness

Family Welfare Association

501 Kingsland Road
London E8 4AU

01–254 6251

Support groups in the London area for young
mothers and families in distress.

Outsiders Club

PO Box 42B
London W1A 42B

01–741 3332

Social events for those isolated by emotional
and physical disability.

Mental health

Good Practices in Mental Health

380–384 Harrow Road
London W9 2HU

01–289 2034

Information on local mental health services.

MIND

22 Harley Street
London W12 2ED

01–637 0741

The National Association for Mental Health.
Information and advice.

Phobias

Phobics Society

4 Cheltenham Road
Chorlton-cum-Hardy
Manchester M21 1QN

061–881 1937

Practical help to overcome phobias.

Psychotherapy

Arbours Association

41A Weston Park
London N8 7BU

01–340 7646

Psychotherapy for emotional distress, providing a 'listening ear' telephone service.

Brent Consultation Centre

Johnston House
51 Winchester Avenue
London NW6 7TT

01–328 0918

A free counselling service for young people aged 12–16. Individual psychotherapy for those who live, work or study in Brent.

British Association of Psychotherapy

121 Hendon Lane
London N3 3P3

01–346 1747

Treatment for those having difficult interpersonal relationships.

Institute of Behaviour Therapy

38 Queen Anne Street
London W1M 9LB

01–346 9646

Treats anxiety and depression.

Relaxation

British Wheel of Yoga

Grafton Grange
Grafton
North Yorkshire YO5 9QQ

090 12 3386

Provides list of qualified yoga teachers.

City Relaxation Consultancy

84 Albany Road
Sittingbourne
Kent ME10 1EL

0795 71834

Courses, talks and industrial consultation for stress management and relaxation.

Relaxation for Living

29 Burwood Park Road
Walton-on-Thames
Surrey KT12 5LH

Relaxation classes and correspondence course. Publishes leaflets and tapes. Send large s.a.e. for information

Yoga for Health Foundation

Ickwell Park
Northill
Nr Biggleswade
Bedfordshire SG18 9EF

Northill (076 727) 271/604/735

Has a residential centre offering stress control, using relaxation techniques.

Self-help

Association of Self-help and Community Groups

7 Chesham Terrace
London W13 9HX

01–579 5589

Runs courses for people who want to set up self-help groups.

Stress

Lifeskills Ltd

3 Brighton Road
London N2 8JU

01–346 9646

Books, tapes and seminars on handling stress.

Organization for Parents Under Stress

29 Newmarket Way
Hornchurch
Essex RM12 6DR

04024 51538

Stress Foundation

Cedar House
Yalding
Kent ME18 6JD

0622 814431

Information, advice and short courses for
managers and trainers.

Stress Research and Control Centre

Department of Occupational Psychology
Birkbeck College
University of London
Malet Street
London WC1E 7HX

01–580 6622

01–631 6243

Researches into stress causes and prevention,
and provides a service to groups and
individuals.

Training

Angela Stern and Associates
(Stress counselling in industry)

11 Palmer Street
London SW1 0AB

01–222 1181

In-house and open courses and seminars.

ASLIB

Information House
26–27 Boswell Street
London WC1N 3JZ

01–430 2671

Occasional stress courses for those in
information management.

Don Taylor and Associates Ltd
(Consulting industrial psychologists)

Old Manor House
Venture Road
Chilworth
Southampton SO1 7NP

0703 760639

Seminars and individual counselling on stress
management.

Eleanor MacDonald Courses Ltd

4 Mapledale Avenue
Croydon CR0 5TA

01–654 4659

Confidence building and personal effectiveness,
with workshop sessions related to stress control.

Greater London Association for Pre-retirement

St Margaret Patten's Church
Eastcheap
London EC3M 1HS

01–623 6630

Professional consultancy for organizers of pre-
retirement courses.

Industrial Society

Robert Hyde House
48 Bryanston Square
London W1H 7LN

01–262 2401

Courses and conferences on stress and related
subjects.

Industrial Society

Pepperell Unit
Robert Hyde House
48 Bryanston Square
London W1H 7LN

01–262 2401

Courses and workshops on all aspects of stress
management.

Jacky Underwood

1 Briavels Close
Montpelier
Bristol BS5 5JJ

0272 542473

Short courses and personal consultations for
managers under pressure.

John Langford Training

30 Tavistock Road
Sheffield S7 1GG

0742 581400

Stress management for organizations and
individuals, including stress levels, coping and
support structures for change.

Leimon Taylor Consultants

9 Somerset Place
Glasgow G3 7JT

041–333 9576

Courses on stress management in organizations.

Careers and Personal Development Associates Ltd

Career Development Centre
77 Morland Road
Addiscombe
Croydon CR0 6EA

01–654 4659

Provides lists of books, tapes and addresses on managing stress effectively.

Options

19 Belmont Road
Twickenham
Middlesex TW2 5DA

01–755 0133

Personal career development counselling and stress management programme design.

Raphael Centre

Hollander Park
Coldharbour Lane
Hildenborough
Tonbridge
Kent TN11 9LE

0732 833924

Residential centre for individual stress management.

Ron Clements Associates

17 Winchfield Court
Pole Lane
Winchfield
Hants RG27 8BL

025126 4321

Wide interest in stress management and particularly in managers' identifying of stress in their staff.

Skills with People

15 Liberia Road
London N15 1JP

01–359 2370

All aspects of interpersonal skills training, including assertiveness, counselling and stress.

Stress Centres Ltd

101 Harley Street
London W1N 1DF

01–935 1811

Courses related to all aspects of stress.

Women and Training Group

GLOSCAT
Oxstalls House
Gloucester GL2 9HW

0542 426836/7

Workshops and publications related to stress and interpersonal skills.

Training materials and aids

Contents

Booklets

How do you drive yourself?

Assesses the limit to which an individual can go without becoming overstressed.

Stress Foundation
Cedar House
Yalding
Kent ME18 6JD

How to prevent stress in everyday life

Ten points for stress prevention.

Stress Foundation
Cedar House
Yalding
Kent ME18 6JD

Staying relaxed
McKnight, R.

A collection of relaxation techniques.

Learning Project Press
14 Walnut Hill
Ardmore
PA 19003
USA

Stress
Lancaster, Dr R.

A detailed look at the causes of, and responses of the body and mind to, stress.

Video Arts Ltd
Dumbarton House
68 Oxford Street
London W1N 9LA
01-637 7288

Stress, tiredness and sleep

Investigates the link between sleep and stress.

Stress Foundation
Cedar House
Yalding
Kent ME18 6JD

The use and abuse of stress

Assesses the balance between too much and too little stress.

Stress Foundation
Cedar House
Yalding
Kent ME18 6JD

What is stress?

Physiological definition of stress.

Stress Foundation
Cedar House
Yalding
Kent ME18 6JD

Why does stress cause illness?

Physiological answer to the above question.

Stress Foundation
Cedar House
Yalding
Kent ME18 6JD

Your personal stress assessment guide

To help individuals determine the amount of stress they are under.

Stress Foundation
Cedar House
Yalding
Kent ME18 6JD

Inventories

Burnout
Jones, J. E. and Brearley, W. L.

A self-applied questionnaire assessing the degree of burnout in an individual.

Organization Design and Development, Inc.
101 Bryn Mawr Avenue
Suite 310
Bryn Mawr
PA 19010
USA

Personal Stress Assessment Inventory (PSAI)
Kindler, Herbert S.

To help an individual maximise benefits from a stress management programme.

Center for Management Effectiveness
PO Box 1202
Pacific Palisades
CA 90272
USA

Courses

Positive stress management

One-week residential course designed for individuals under stress, providing them with effective stress management techniques. Held twice yearly (Nov, Apr). £760 + VAT.

Roffey Park Management College
Forest Road
Horsham
West Sussex RH11 4TD
029383 644

Coping with stress

Two–day course for managers wishing to control stress in employees and bring about more effective performance.
Held twice yearly (Nov, Feb).

Guardian Business Services
119 Farringdon Road
London EC1R 3DA
01–278 6787

Coping with stress

Three-day course for managers to introduce
practices of preventive health management.
Held annually (Feb). £100.

Burton Manor College
Burton
South Wirral
Cheshire L64 5SJ
051-336 5172

Managing the pressures!

One-day stress and time-management
workshop for managers to identify home and
work pressures and develop an action plan to
manage stress positively. £138 + VAT.

Pepperell Unit
Industrial Society
Robert Hyde House
48 Bryanston Square
London W1H 7LH
01–262 2401

Management of stress

Four-day residential workshop to teach how to
effectively manage stress.
Held twice yearly (Nov, Feb). £570 + VAT.

Fielden House Productivity Centre
856 Wilmslow Road
Didsbury
Manchester M20 8RY
061–445 2426

Managing stress

One-day briefings by Dr Audrey Livingstone
Booth

Invicta Training
6 Broadway
Catford
London SE6 4SP
01–690 9931

The management of stress at work

Two-day residential course for middle and
senior management in medium to large
organizations, and for safety and personnel
managers.
Held twice yearly (Sept, Apr). £150 approx.

Loughborough University of Technology
Centre for Extension Studies
Loughborough
Leicestershire LE11 3TU
0509 263171

Manage your stress

One-day in-company workshop or seven half-
hour self-study sessions teaching self-
regulatory techniques for stress management.

McGraw-Hill International Training Systems
(UK) Ltd
Shoppenhangers Road
Maidenhead
Berks SL6 2QL
0628 23432

Relaxation therapy

Ten one-hour sessions for London workers
prone to stress. Courses are run in-company.

City Relaxation Consultancy
84 Albany Road
Sittingbourne
Kent ME10 1EL
0795 71835

Stress: The trainer's course

Four-day course for Training Officers wishing
to introduce stress management training
programmes.
Held annually (July). £395.

Brunel Institute of Organization and Social
Studies
Brunel University
Uxbridge
Middlesex UB8 3PH
0895 56461

Videos and films

*Be well: The later years. Stress in the later
years*

24-minute video/16mm film examines stress
and the elderly – bereavement, retirement etc.
Introduces coping skills and suggestions.

Boulton-Hawker Films Ltd
28 George Street
Hadleigh
Ipswich
Suffolk IP7 5BG
0473 822235

Bitter wages

37-minute video, made in 1984, examines the
stressors of work which particularly affect
women. Designed for use with women's
groups and trades unions.

Cinema of Women Films
31 Clerkenwell Close
London EC1R 0AT
01-251 4978

The counselling interview

Spells out the four key stages to a good counselling interview: setting up the interview; encouraging people to talk; helping them think it through; letting them find the solution.

Video Arts Ltd
Dumbarton House
68 Oxford Street
London W1N 9LA
01-637 7288

Education for adults: Learning in groups

Of particular interest to Trainers, this 1985 24-minute video looks at two facilitators working with a group on stress control.

Open University Film Library
Open University Educational Enterprises
12 Cofferidge Close
Stony Stratford
Milton Keynes
Bucks MK11 1BY
0908 566744

Health choices: No. 2 – How do you achieve it?

14-minute video made in 1981, examines individual strategies for coping with stressful situations.

Northamptonshire Area Health Authority CCTV Unit
Video Communication Services
Beaumont
Cliftonville
Northampton NN1 5DN
0604 37853

Helping to cope with bereavement

29-minute video, made in 1984, with accompanying notes investigates different forms of bereavement, involving a wide range of related issues.

Milestone TTV Ltd
Field House
Field Lane
Aberford
West Yorks LS25 3AE
0532 754988

How to last a lifetime

Five 30-minute video films, made in 1984, investigate stress under the following titles:

1. Facing the problems
2. Recognising yourself
3. Working for survival
4. Learning to live
5. Taking control

Guild Sound and Vision
6 Royce Road
Peterborough PE1 5YB
0733 315315

How to survive the 9 to 5

41-minute video made in 1985, examines stress, its effects and causes in the workplace in Britain today. Cary Cooper looks at the state of the art in stress control, social relationships, and the impact of changing attitudes and employment.

Thames TV International
Alexa Dalby
149 Tottenham Court Road
London W1P 9LL
01-387 9494

The life that's left

30-minute video/16mm colour film, made in 1977, shows how grief from bereavement should be acknowledged and not stifled.

CTVC
Beeson's Yard
Bury Lane
Rickmansworth
Herts WD3 1DS
0923 77793

Living with stress

26-minute video/16mm colour film shows how individuals must find personal ways of handling stress.

Edward Patterson Associates
Treetops
Cannongate Road
Hythe
Kent CT21 5PT
0303 64195

Managing stress

34-minute 16mm colour film identifies causes and effects of stress and reviewing stress management techniques.

Gower/TFI
Gower House
Croft Road
Aldershot
Hampshire GU11 3HR
0252 331551

One in five

20-minute video/16mm colour film shows how to spot early warning signs of impending coronary trouble and take preventive action by modifying life-style accordingly.

Millbank Films
Thames House
Millbank
London SW1P 3JF
01-839 7176

The parting

16-minute 16mm colour film shows how a small community deals with the death of a member.

Concord Films Council
201 Felixstowe Road
Ipswich
Suffolk IP3 9BJ
0473 76012

People can change – an introduction to counselling and therapy

38-minute video, made in 1982, includes a short history of the growth of counselling and therapy, discussions between therapists and clients; points concerning availability within the NHS are raised.

Concord Films Council
201 Felixstowe Road
Ipswich
Suffolk IP3 9BJ
0473 76012

Pressure principle

25-minute video/16mm colour film shows how to recognise and treat stress, tension and depression.

BNA Communications Europe
17 Dartmouth Street
London SW1H 9BL
01-222 8834

Problems with alcohol

33-minute video, made in 1986, considers the treatment of alcohol problems with reference to co-counselling and groupwork.

University of Sheffield Audio-Visual and TV Centre
Sheffield
S10 2TN
0742 768555

Relaxation and biofeedback

35-minute b/w video, made in 1976, to teach medical students, nurses, psychologists etc techniques of relaxation and where these techniques would be useful.

BMA Film Library
BMA House
Tavistock Square
London WC1H 9JP
01-388 7976 (ext 317)

The smoking video

13-minute video, made in 1986, showing discussion with smokers and ex-smokers with a view to helping people stop smoking. For sale only.

Groves Medical Audio-Visual Library
Holly House
220 New London Road
Chelmsford
Essex CM2 9BJ
0245 283351

Someone like you

Complete trainer's pack including a 19-minute video made for the Post Office on how to recognise the abuse of alcohol. Available for purchase or hire.

Mr Ramsaran
The Post Office
Room 94
33 Grosvenor Place
London SW1X 1PX
01-245 7358

Someone to talk to

Five 26-minute videos discuss the nature and effect of depression.

Guild Sound and Vision
6 Royce Road
Peterborough PE1 5YB
0733 315315

Stress

30-minute video/16mm colour film mainly aimed at those responsible for coping with stress in others.

CTVC Film Library
Hillside
Merry Hill Road
Bushey
Herts WD2 1DR
01-950 4426

Stress

25-minute 16mm colour film, made in 1985, looks at the problem of stress by means of a drama documentary profiling a highly stressed executive.

Video Arts Ltd
Dumbarton House
68 Oxford Street
London W1N 9LA
01-637 7288

Stress at work

24-minute video points out features of occupational stress

British Medical Association
Film Library
BMA House
Tavistock Square
London WC1H 9JP
01-388 7976 (ext 317)

Stress at work

Videodisc commissioned by the MSC as part of a training effort aimed at its own staff on the subject of stress at work.

BBC Open University Production Centre
Milton Keynes
MK7 6BH
0908 655337

Stress in industry

16-minute colour videocassette aimed at employers showing a scheme of Plessy Connectors to deal with stress in the workforce.

Northamptonshire Area Health Authority
39 Billing Road
Northampton NN1 5BA
0604 37853

The stress manager

Pack of three audio tapes and a book to identify stress and causes of stress and to build a stress management action plan.

Time Manager International
50 High Street
Henley in Arden
Solihull
West Midlands B95 5AN
05642 4100

Stress – Parents with a handicapped child

30-minute video/16mm film, made in 1964, examines the stress in five families where there is a handicapped child.

Concord Films Council
201 Felixstowe Road
Ipswich
Suffolk IP3 9BJ
0473 76012

That's the limit

A series of five 10-minute videos, made in 1985, shows how alcohol intake affects lives and how to drink in moderation and stay healthy.

Guild Sound and Video
6 Royce Road
Peterborough PE1 5YB
0733 315315

Time's right: A look ahead to retirement

5-minute video/16mm film, made in 1984, encourages people to plan their retirement and not to see it as a retirement from life.

Concord Films Council
201 Felixstowe Road
Ipswich
Suffolk IP3 9BJ
0473 76012

Till death us do part

30-minute video looks, by talking to recently bereaved men and women, at the problems of bereavement.

Concord Films Council
201 Felixstowe Road
Ispwich
Suffolk IP3 9BJ
0473 76012

Turnaround – A story of recovery

47-minute 16mm film, made in 1985, shows a group of alcoholic and drug dependant women in a Canadian treatment centre. The film shows the crises causing the dependence and the struggle to come to terms with the disease.

Concord Films Council
201 Felixstowe Road
Ipswich
Suffolk IP3 9BJ
0473 76012

Well woman

Series of 30-minute videos, made in 1983, offers a positive approach to women's health. The advice of women with experience of problems is frequently featured.

Concord Films Council
201 Felixstowe Road
Ipswich
Suffolk IP3 9BJ
0473 76012

We're O.K.

9-minute 16 mm animated film, made in 1975, aimed at improving interpersonal relationships.

Concord Films Council
201 Felixstowe Road
Ipswich
Suffolk IP3 9BJ
0473 76012

When I say no, I feel guilty

30-minute training film, made in 1978, introduces assertiveness training using case studies and role playing exercises.

Gower/TFI
Gower House
Croft Road
Aldershot
Hampshire GU11 3HR
0252 331551

Work is a four-letter word

41-minute video looks at occupational stress and its management. The film gives practical advice on job satisfaction.

Guild Sound and Video
6 Royce Road
Peterborough PE1 5YB
0733 315315

Working with difficult people

25-minute video/16mm film, made in 1984,
shows how to come to terms with an
aggressor and aggression and how to cope
with aggressive behaviour.

Gower/TFI
Gower House
Croft Road
Aldershot
Hampshire GU11 3HR
0252 331551

Section 5.
Bibliography and stress studies

Contents

Introduction

Arrangement

An extensive general bibliography on stress is included in *Understanding Stress – Part One*. The bibliography included here is taken from that book and features publications and articles relevant to the role of the Trainer. A selection of stress studies is also included.

Readers and researchers who wish to find more in-depth material are directed to 'Other sources' at the end of this listing.

Entries

Each entry includes:

- author/editor
- title
- publisher
- date of publication
- ISBN – where allocated

Many entries also include a brief summary to help you decide if the title is useful for needs.

1. Role of the Trainer

Interpersonal Skills

ACKROYD, A. (ed.)
Training counselling
British Association for Counselling
1984
0946181136

Lists counselling training courses available in the UK

COOPER, C. L. (ed.)
Improving interpersonal relations: some approaches to social skills training
Gower
1981
056602277X

COOPER, G., CRAWFORD, C. et al.
Trainers in counselling
British Association for Counselling
1984
094618111X

Lists Trainers specialising in counselling. Loose leaf format with an amendment service.

HONEY, P.
Face-to-face: a practical guide to interactive skills
Institute of Personnel Management
1976
085292142X

INSKIPP, F.
A manual for Trainers: resource book for setting up and running counselling courses
Alexia Publications
1985
0951095005

PAUL, N.
'Assertiveness without tears: a training programme for executive equality'
Personnel Management
Vol. 11, no. 41
April 1979
pp 37–40

Strategies

BOND, M. and KILTY, J.
Practical methods of dealing with stress
Human Potential Research Project, Department of Educational Studies, University of Surrey
1982
1852370114

Resource material and workshop outlines.

BOOT, N. BUCLE, A. and PERKINS, E.
The stress pack
Nottingham and Bassetlaw Health Education Unit
1986

A pack for Trainers to use with individuals and groups. Includes OHP slides and handouts.

The cost of stress: summary of a one-day workshop
Women in Training, c/o Department of Management Studies,
Gloucestershire College of Arts and Technology, Oxstalls Lane, Gloucester
GL2 9HW
1984

Includes papers on the cost of stress, causes, managerial stress and coping.

COX, S.
Change and stress in the modern office
Further Education Unit/Pickup, Department of Education and Science
1986
0948621427

Analyses the changing office environment and identifies training needs and solutions.

Counselling for resettlement: dealing with stress
Training Section, Agricultural and Food Research Council
September 1986

Defines stress and suggests coping skills.

McCLEAN, A. A.
Work stress
Addison Wesley
1979
0201045923

ORLANS, V.
'The Trainer's role in stress management and prevention'
Journal of European and Industrial Training
Vol. 10, no. 5, 1986
pp 3–5

Examines effects of workplace stress and absenteeism. Suggests training programmes should analyse individual/occupational/ organizational stressors and play a proactive role in managing stress.

2. Stress studies

Stress research in the Civil Service

The Civil Service Occupational Health Service (CSOHS) has been interested in stress in the Civil Service for some years and has helped conduct, or been associated with, a number of research projects. A good deal of the data which is so often quoted, in this context was derived from the so-called 'Whitehall Study' set up in 1968 to look into factors which prevent cardio-respiratory disease in male civil servants. This involved some 18,000 men aged 40 to 64. It was followed up in 1978 by a study involving 1,200 male and female employees in the Department of the Environment.

The most interesting finding was that those at greater risk from illnesses which are thought to be stress-related – primarily coronary heart disease and raised blood pressure – were the lower level civil servants at messengerial and clerical level. Messengers had a coronary heart disease rate 3.6 times that of those in the higher Civil Service, and this was not adequately explained by other factors like differences in smoking habits.

Other recent research has been carried out by Professor Cary Cooper of University of Manchester Institute of Science and Technology into stress among Tax Officers (Higher Grade) in the Inland Revenue. This research was primarily conducted for the Inland Revenue Staff Federation. It suggested that Tax Officers are more prone to anxiety and depression, than those at comparable levels in other professions.

The CSOHS is currently helping Professor Michael Marmot of the Department of Community Medicine in the University College Hospital Medical School conduct an extended study in six departments of stress-related problems and different approaches to dealing with them.

General

CHERRY, N.
'Nervous strain, anxiety and symptoms amongst 32-year-old men at work in Britain'
Journal of Occupational Psychology
Vol. 57, no. 2, 1984
pp 95–105.

GILES, E.
Stress and the personal director: a preliminary investigation
1985

A research project which includes questionnaires and a bibliography.

Apply Murray Giles Associates, 1 Rectory Place, Hawkswood Lane, Chislehurst, Kent BR7 5PN.

MCDERMOTT, D.
'Professional burnout and its relation to job characteristics, satisfactions and control'
Journal of Human Stress
Vol. 10, no. 2, Summer 1984
pp 79–85

A study which examines work burnout among 104 professionals. Concludes that there is significant correlation between the amount of work control by the individual and burnout.

ORLANS, V. and SHIPLEY, P.
A survey of stress management and prevention facilities in a sample of UK organizations
Department of Occupational Psychology, Birkbeck College, University of London
1983

Examines stress control in 35 organizations with particular focus on training and welfare. Concludes that only a few tackle stress directly with the emphasis on management rather than prevention.

Industry

BURKE, R. J.
'Are you fed up with work?'
Personnel Administration
Vol. 34, no. 1, January/February 1971
pp 27–31

Identifies methods of managing job tensions among supervisors of engineering personnel.

FRASER, R.
The incidence of neurosis among factory workers
HMSO
Report no. 90, Industrial Health Research Board, Medical Research Council
1947

Examines the incidence of neurosis among 3,000 employees in light and medium engineering factories, over a six-month period. Work factors emerge as being an important cause of neurotic illness.

MARSHALL, J. and COOPER, C. L. (ed.)
Coping with stress at work: case studies from industry
Gower
1981
0566023385

An account of how different organizations are responding to the effects of stress, including training, relaxation, organizational structure etc.

Service organizations (including the Civil Service)

COOPER, C. L.
'Stress in the Police Service'
Journal of Occupational Medicine
Vol. 24, no. 9, 1982
pp 653–655

COOPER, C. L.
Mental health and satisfaction among Tax Officers
Department of Management Sciences. UMIST
1984/5

Assessed the mental well-being of 318 tax officers. Found that an autocratic management style predicted job dissatisfaction.

CRUMP, J., COOPER, C. L. and MAXWELL, V. B.
'Stress among Air Traffic Controllers: Occupational sources of coronary heart disease risk'
Journal of Occupational Behaviour
Vol. 2, no. 4, 1981
pp 293–303

FARBER, B. A.
Stress and burnout in the human service professions
Pergamon Press
1983
0080288014

A preliminary study of stress in the Police Service: Conclusions and recommendations as submitted to the Association of Chief Police Officers working party on police stress
SRDB Human Factors Group, Home Office.
1983.
Final report of a workshop series which includes management systems, styles and support.

'Stress in the medical laboratory'
Medical Laboratory Sciences
Vol. 43, Supplement 1, October 1986
pp 583–84
Biochemistry Department
St. Vincents Hospital, Elm Park, Dublin 4

Measures occupational stress of hospital personnel. Finds that very small and very large laboratories are equally stressful.

ZALEZNIK, A. et al.
'Stress reactions in organisations: Syndrome, causes and consequences'
Behavioural Science
Vol. 22, no. 3, May 1977
pp 151–162

A study of stress among 2,000 individuals in a large organization in Canada.

Women

COOPER, C. L. and DAVIDSON, M. J.
High pressure: working lives of women managers
Fontana
1982
0006362362

Suggests that women managers have major additional stressors to cope with at work and at home.

COOPER, C. L. and DAVIDSON, M. J.
Stress and the woman manager
Robertson
1983
0855206233

Compares managerial men and women and concludes that, while women can help themselves, direct action is required in organizations on recruitment, training and career counselling.

HAYNES, S. G. and FEINLEIB, M.
'Women, work and coronary heart disease'
American Journal of Public Health
Vol. 70, no. 2, 1980
pp 133–141

TUNG, R. L.
'Comparative analysis of the occupational stress profiles of male versus female administrators'
Journal of Vocational Behaviour
Vol. 17, 1980
pp 344–355

A study which suggests that female administrators experience substantially lower levels of self-perceived work stress than their male counterparts.

3. Other sources

There are a number of organizations offering bibliographic information. Two we have found particularly useful are:

1. ACAS
   Work Research Unit
   St Vincent House
   30 Orange Street
   London WC2H 7HH
   01–839 9281

Publishes a bibliography entitled *Workplace stress* with regular updates. Non-annotated.

2. John Chittock
   37 Gower Street
   London WC1E 6HH
   01–580 2842

Publishes *Stress: a resources file,* which includes courses, publications and research.

Printed in the United Kingdom for Her Majesty's Stationery Office
Dd289879   C20   11.87   3936   12521